WELCOME
TO THE
REAL WORKING
WORLD

What Every
Employee
Must Know
To Succeed

FRANK G. DOERGER

Publisher: W. Quay Hays
Editorial Director: Peter Hoffman
Editor: Amy Spitalnick
Art Director: Susan Anson
Production Director: Trudihope Schlomowitz

For information:
General Publishing Group, Inc.
2701 Ocean Park Boulevard
Santa Monica, CA 90405

Library of Congress Cataloging-in-Publication Data

Doerger, Frank G.
   Welcome to the real working world : everything you must know to
succeed / by Frank G. Doerger.
        p.   cm.
   Includes index.
   ISBN 1-57544-052-0
   1. Career development. I. Title
HF5381.D523   1997
650.1—dc21   97-4950
                                                          CIP

Printed in the USA by RR Donnelley & Sons Company
10 9 8 7 6 5 4 3 2 1

General Publishing Group
Los Angeles

< *Table of Contents* >

< *Acknowledgments* >

This book grew out of innumerable conversations I forced upon family, friends, coworkers, and even strangers. Many patient people shared their ideas and knowledge with me. More importantly, they encouraged me to write this book.

My sincerest thanks to Howard Wells for educating me about the book-publishing industry. Although he may disagree, I doubt this book would have been published without his support, guidance, and enviable editing skills. Many thanks to Suzy, my wife, and to Al Eilers and Mike Gramaglia, my good friends, for their many insights.

My appreciation to Betsy, my fifteen-year-old daughter, for immediately coming to my rescue again and again when I needed help getting organized or making photocopies. My thanks to Mike Werner, Mara Whitman, and Margaret Rieger for their encouragement.

Very special thanks to Scott, my seventeen-year-old son, for his confidence and support. He spent many hours actively listening to me ramble on about ideas for this book. He also displayed endless patience as he tutored me on the many features of word processing software. In addition, his keen eyes spied typo after typo that somehow found their way into each succeeding draft.

Of course, I am indebted to Mr. Quay Hays and all the helpful people at General Publishing Group for making this book possible.

< *Is This Book for You?* >

Work is much more fun than fun.
—NOEL COWARD

Perhaps you're trying to land your first "real job." Perhaps you've just entered the world of work and aren't quite comfortable with your new role. Perhaps you've been employed for some time and want to polish your business and social skills. If so, this book was written for you. It will help you perform better in any job by:

> Giving you an idea of the many situations you'll face. **It will help you sidestep the pitfalls experienced by workplace rookies.**

> Giving you a quick-reference tool. **It will help you quickly and easily find practical answers to real-world problems.**

> Making you more confident and efficient. **It will help you get promoted.**

This is not a textbook filled with theory and lengthy chapters. It's a handbook. If you don't know what to say when your boss compliments you, spend two minutes with this book and be ready the next time. If you're asked to lead a meeting, turn to the chapter on meetings and start preparing. Better yet, browse through it now so you're ready when your chance to shine comes.

Work is a necessity for man. Man invented the alarm clock.
—PABLO PICASSO

< *Introduction* >

If you're going to play the game properly, you'd better know every rule.
—BARBARA JORDAN

Choosing a career, finding a job, fitting in, and developing a professional self has challenged every generation of workers. Recently it has become more difficult than ever. Why? **Here are some of the reasons why finding and then keeping a good job have become so challenging:**

> **The world economy is changing.** Competition isn't restricted to local, state, or national boundaries. It's a global economy, and U.S. companies must compete with foreign companies that may have lower wage rates or benefit from their governments' subsidies.

> **The U.S. economy is changing.** It's moving from a manufacturing to a service- and knowledge-based economy. This means that jobs that are relatively easy to learn, such as making and moving things in a factory, are disappearing. They are being replaced by jobs that require working with ideas and with people, many of diverse backgrounds.

> **Our society is changing.** Parents and educators often don't have the time, energy, or knowledge to teach the interpersonal skills valued by employers in a complex, global economy.

> **Organizations are changing.** They want (and need) to be lean and nimble and react quickly to economic, competitive, and technological changes. They want to get the job done with fewer employees. They are decentralizing and "flattening" themselves.

> **The skills employers value are changing.** They expect more from employees than just following orders and working hard. They want people who can communicate well, generate ideas and solutions, take the initiative, quickly learn new skills, recognize and seize opportunities, lead, and teach.

> **Jobs are changing.** Personal computers have revamped the way most work is done. Using them has become a necessity for many jobs.

> Landing a good job, keeping it, and advancing in it isn't as easy as it once was. Our service-based economy has many low-paying jobs. **Competition is fierce for good-paying positions that require higher levels of communication and interpersonal skills.**

> **Employers are less willing to hold on to marginally productive workers, regardless of age or longevity.** Promotions go to those who project the right image, get things done, and work well with others.

Welcome to the Real Working World can improve your chances of succeeding in this new economy. It presents numerous practical techniques and tips to help you anticipate and overcome the many challenges you'll face during your years on the job.

Good luck!

> *There is no happiness except in the realization*
> *that we have accomplished something.*
> —HENRY FORD

GETTING STARTED

< *Cover Letters and Résumés* >

I cannot agree with those who rank modesty among the virtues.
—SHERLOCK HOLMES (SIR ARTHUR CONAN DOYLE)

The purpose of the cover letter and résumé is to obtain an interview with a potential employer. It should make the employer want to meet and learn more about you. Some tips:

> **The cover letter should be written as specifically as possible for the company and position you seek.** Do your best to address the cover letter to a specific person in the company.

> The cover letter should make it obvious that you know a great deal about the company and the position. Information is often available from public libraries, chambers of commerce, and corporate public relations departments.

> **The résumé must be attractive to the eye and to the touch.** Use 20- or 24-pound 100 percent cotton bond paper. Have a one-inch margin around the borders. Use lots of white space to make it easy to read. Use a laser printer, good typewriter, or letter-quality printer.

> **The cover letter and résumé must be flawless—no typos, misspelled words, or grammatical errors.** Ask someone to do the proofreading honors to make sure.

> Center your name, address, and phone number at the top of the page. **Exclude personal information** such as age, height, weight, marital status, and number of children. These are irrelevant to your ability to do the job.

> List your education first if the position you are seeking requires special training. If it doesn't, list your education after your work experience. If you think that you may appear to be overeducated for the position, consider listing your advanced education under a topic like Special Interests.

> **Decide which résumé type is best for you:** chronological, functional, or a combination.

  • **The chronological style** should cover no more than your last ten years of employment. Begin with your current position and work backward. List the employer, your position, and dates of employment, and then emphasize your accomplishments. Try to include numbers in describing your achievements. For instance, "I increased sales by 30 percent," or "I managed a department of twenty-five." You may want to avoid this style if you've been with your most recent employer for an extended time, or if you've had gaps in your employment.

  • **The functional style** is useful if you've been in the same job for a long time. Instead of listing employment history, list the skills you've acquired and how you've used them to the benefit of your employer.

> If your work history includes several employers, with increasing responsibilities and good results, list each employer and what you've accomplished for them.

> **Don't mention salary** because it may exclude you from consideration if your current pay is much less or much more than the prospective employer has in mind.

> **No need to say references are available on request—that is understood.** However, keep handy a list of personal and professional references. Never submit a reference without first getting approval. You may want to give a copy of your résumé to your references to make sure they are up to date on your accomplishments.

The trouble with unemployment
is that the minute you wake up in the morning you're on the job.
—SLAPPY WHITE

< *Interviewing for a Job* >

If you tell the truth,
you don't have to remember anything.
—MARK TWAIN

The purpose of the job interview goes beyond getting hired. Use it to demonstrate to a potential employer the contribution you can make to the success of the company. Use it to learn what opportunities this employer can provide for your professional and personal growth.

Prepare carefully for the job interview so you and the employer can make the right decisions about your future. If your research convinces you that you'd like to be associated with this company, you must demonstrate this belief in the interview. **Your attitude is vital**—it's been said that 85 percent of effective communication is attitude and body language.

> **Do your homework.** Find out as much about the company, department, and interviewer as you can. Identify how you can make a contribution to the company. Know what you are looking for in the way of growth and development. Above all—be specific. Give examples.

> Get a good idea of how long it will take to get to where the interview will be held. **Know where to park and how to get to the meeting place.** Consider making a trial run a few days before the interview. If you are unsure of the logistics, call the prospective employer and find out.

> **Decide well in advance what to wear.** Make sure you have clean clothes and polished shoes. Wear clothes consistent with the industry, company, and position.

> **Arrive about ten minutes before the meeting time.** If you are asked to wait, be polite but not chummy toward those you see while waiting.

> **Be friendly and considerate to everyone.** A complimentary word about you from the receptionist, secretary, or anyone else you meet while on the company's premises could tilt the scales in your favor.

> Stand and shake hands with the interviewer, and immediately thank them for inviting you to talk.

> Sit only after you've been invited to.

> Do not address the interviewer by first name unless you are asked to.

> Have a businesslike pen and notepad ready for note taking.

> Avoid fidgeting or fiddling with your pen, briefcase, or purse. **Sit up straight, and look directly at the interviewer.**

> Do not touch the interviewer's desk or anything on it. Refrain from looking as if you are trying to read anything on the desk.

> Reply in a strong, clear voice. **Make positive statements.** Avoid rambling. Don't bad-mouth your current employer, its employees, or competitors.

> **Rehearse—perhaps into a tape recorder—answering versions of these commonly asked questions:**
  - How's the weather?
  - Tell me a little about yourself.
  - What do you do in your current job? Why do you want to leave it?
  - What did you enjoy about the jobs you've had? What did you dislike?
  - What did you achieve in your previous jobs?
  - What are your strengths? Weaknesses?
  - Describe your ideal job.
  - What would you like to be doing five years from now?
  - Why do you think we should hire you for this position?
  - What are you doing now to improve yourself?
  - How much money do you expect to earn?

> Don't give the impression that you will accept any job with any employer. Your mission is to determine if this job opportunity is right for you.

> **Be confident.** Remember, you're evaluating the company and position also. You're looking for a good fit. **Ask questions, for example:**
  - Why is this position open?
  - What are the primary responsibilities of this position?
  - How will this position change in the next few years?
  - What is the next logical career move?
  - How are employees selected for promotion?
  - When and how will my performance be evaluated?

> **Have examples**—with numbers—of what you've accomplished in the past.

> If you feel good about the position, say so with enthusiasm and add "I won't let you down." **Sell yourself.**

> Don't bring up the topic of salary right away—your first concern is what you will be doing in the position, as well as its opportunities. However, don't let the interview end without at least a mention of pay range.

> Before you leave, make sure to mention your strong interest in the position. Smile, shake hands, and exit quickly and confidently.

> **Immediately after the interview, make notes about what was said.** You may want to write down names and other details. Consider using a tape recorder so you'll remember important facts.

> **Write a letter thanking the interviewer** for seeing you. Make sure you have the correct spelling of all names. If you're unsure of a spelling, call the company and find out. Make sure to express strong interest in the position.

> If you receive a letter of rejection, let the interviewer know you would be interested in talking again if another position opens.

It's great to be great, but it's greater to be human.
—WILL ROGERS

< *Career Choices* >

*Choose your rut carefully—
you're going to be in it for the next ten miles.*
—SIGN ON A MUDDY ROAD IN TENNESSEE

Some people are born lucky. They seem to know from age six exactly how they want to earn a living and how to go about finding the right job. Others seem to just effortlessly fall into a job they love. Then there are those who are not so lucky. They move from one unrewarding job to another.

How you'll spend the majority of your waking hours is too important to leave to blind luck. **Here's an approach to finding your life's work:**

> **Look inside.** Don't study the job market and then try to shape yourself to fit a slot. First, study yourself. What do you enjoy doing, thinking about, talking about, and reading about? Pursue your interests. Answer the call of those natural talents that cry out to be used. As interests and talents blossom, career choices often become obvious. Career-guidance professionals can help. Schools and other organizations may provide these services for little or no cost.

> **Ignore others.** Parents, teachers, friends, and society subtly push us to make "acceptable" career choices. Because you're intelligent doesn't mean you should be a physician, lawyer, or similar professional. Because your grandfather and father were lawyers doesn't mean you must carry on the tradition. Seek no one's approval—only you will have to live with your decision. It's better to be a happy

auto mechanic or zookeeper than a brain surgeon living a life of quiet desperation. Trust yourself. Deep down you know what feels right and what doesn't.

> **Study.** Many before you have had similar hopes, dreams, and aspirations. Seek advice from those who've made good career choices. Review the paths they took and then chart your educational and employment course.

> **Play offense.** View work as an opportunity to create something worthwhile, not simply as a way to keep the wolf from the door. Playing defense means allowing your talents and personality to wither while you wonder why financial security or creature comforts seem unrewarding.

> **Don't grow roots.** Chances are you'll be part of an organization. It will have its own personality, values, and purpose. If you find yourself in conflict with these, get out—fast. Don't hope and wait for a magical convergence. While you wait, security, pay, family obligations, inertia, and a pension will become a golden chain attaching you to something you really don't want. You'll feel trapped but stay unhappily put because "it's only fifteen years to retirement."

> **Don't look for peer support.** Many of your coworkers find themselves incapable of pulling themselves out of a rut. Don't seek career guidance from them. And don't expect them to support you in your quest for a more satisfying job. They'll find countless reasons to try to convince you, and themselves, that it's too impractical and risky to seek real job satisfaction.

> **Don't think it's too late.** It's difficult to make the perfect career choice on the first try. If inner satisfaction just isn't there, try again. Ours is an enormous, dynamic economy with innumerable opportunities. Try another fit if necessary. Don't think in terms of a single decision. Be open to the possibility of several, perhaps very different, careers over your lifetime.

> **Do, don't just be.** Becoming an architect, holding an advanced degree, or being a computer expert are not ends. They should be means to a larger end. Decide what you want to accomplish. Help feed the world? Entertain others? Help ease mental suffering? Design earth-friendly products? Decide on your purpose, and then choose the means to best achieve it.

Your work is to discover your work
and then with all your heart to give yourself to it.
—BUDDHA

< *Learning* >

*In the world of the future, the new illiterate
will be the person who has not learned how to learn.*
—Alvin Toffler

Changes come quickly and often in today's workplace. A few years ago, the tools in the average office consisted of a telephone and a typewriter. Now, workers must contend with computers, word processing software, fax machines, voice mail, E-mail, laser printers, electronic spreadsheets, and a variety of other specialized software. Training for using these new tools may be extensive or nonexistent. In either case, employees are asked to take responsibility for their learning. They're expected to learn quickly and become more productive. Learning has become a large part of all jobs. **Learning how to learn is a skill that is essential to good job performance. Here are some tips on learning:**

> **Recognize its importance.** Employers want employees who stay abreast of developments in their industry, profession, company, and job. They want employees who are capable of anticipating and responding to change. The more you're able to learn, the more valuable you'll be to your present, and future, employers.

> **Develop a plan.** Determine what areas you want to study. Consider not only your personal interests but also the skills and knowledge valued by your employer. Does your boss value math skills? Management skills? Writing skills? Computer-programming skills? If you don't know, ask.

> **Use several approaches.** There are many ways to acquire new skills and knowledge. Employers often pay the tuition for classes at local colleges and technical schools. They may also pay for magazine subscriptions and books. Borrowing books, audiotapes, magazines, and videotapes from public libraries is an inexpensive way to increase your knowledge.

> **Join professional or trade organizations.** This gives you a chance to learn from others who do similar work. These organizations usually have informative newsletters, conferences, and magazines. Employers often pay for the dues.

> **Start conversations.** You can learn something from everyone you meet, on and off the job. Listen and learn. Ask questions, and steer the conversation to topics of interest to you. If a person knows a great deal about something, it won't be hard to get them to talk about it.

> **Volunteer.** Community and club volunteer work often provide a wide variety of work-related experiences. This may include public speaking, bookkeeping, event planning, and writing newsletters. Volunteering also provides a good feeling of helping others as you learn.

> **Discover your learning style.** Primary learning styles include reading, listening, watching, question-and-answer sessions, and doing. Use the styles best suited to you. Experts say most of us remember 10 percent of what we read, 20 percent of what we hear, 30 percent of what we see, 50 percent of what we hear and see, 70 percent of what we say and write, and 90 percent of what we say as we do it.

> **Don't become discouraged.** We don't learn in one fell swoop. We go through stages, such as enthusiasm, apprehension, awkwardness, success, plateau, mastery, and realization that there is always much more to learn. Anticipate, and chart your progress through these stages. This will reduce the natural frustrations that arise as you learn.

The next best thing to knowing something
is knowing where to find it.
—SAMUEL JOHNSON

SETTLING IN

< *Expectations* >

If you have a job without aggravations, you don't have a job.
—MALCOLM FORBES

WELCOME TO THE REAL WORLD is a remark young workers often hear during their first few weeks on the job. Old-timers like to say it when a newcomer witnesses a bureaucratic foul-up. It's their way of warning the novice that the world of work may hold a few surprises. **Here are a few "real world" surprises** and tips on how to maintain a positive attitude:

> Goldbricks. **Some employees are experts at stretching four hours of work into an eight-hour day.** They work hard at avoiding work. Don't waste your time wondering how this happens or why it's allowed. Accept it.

> Pay. **Employees doing the same work may be paid different amounts.** Union contracts, longevity, negotiating skills, and the overall job market are contributing factors. In addition, it's been said that workers are underpaid in the first half of their career and overpaid in the second half. Don't fret over a lack of fairness. Concentrate on becoming more valuable to your employer.

> Cliques. **Large groups tend to informally subdivide into smaller, more closely knit groups. Friction may develop between these cliques.** Signs include ignoring one another, uncooperative behavior, and outright hostility. Beware of overzealous members who try to convince you to join their camp. Remain neutral, and try to stay on good terms with all.

> Efficiency. **Your company or department may not run like the well-oiled machine you had expected.** Some old-timers will delight in sharing embarrassing corporate folklore with you. They may embellish the story about the building that was newly painted the day before it was demolished. Others may be quick to tell you about blunders and mistakes as soon as they occur. Expect these stories and the occasional snafu (situation normal all fouled up) as a natural part of any organization. Spend your time improving matters, not pointing out deficiencies.

> Improvements. New employees bring a fresh eye to a department and can often see things overlooked by others. **Don't expect your opinion and ideas to be automatically and warmly received.** First, there is always the possibility you are wrong. Second, when you are right, expect the organization to make changes at its accustomed pace. It may be painfully slow to you, but be patient. Third, good ideas are sometimes rejected. Don't despair or complain. Work with the organization, not against it.

Don't fight forces; use them.
—R. BUCKMINSTER FULLER

< *Reputation* >

I don't want to be liked, I just want to be respected.
—REGGIE JACKSON

Your workplace reputation will be formed quickly. You'll be pegged
with personality traits, such as quiet or talkative, passive or assertive,
friendly or aloof. Above all, you'll want to be considered dependable.
Employers value employees who consistently get the job done. Some
tips on developing such a reputation for reliability:

> **Arrive on time.** Being punctual is one way to demonstrate respect
for your coworkers. If you are unavoidably late, a simple "I'm sorry
I'm late" is appropriate.

> **Return telephone calls and E-mail messages.** The common practice
is to return telephone calls and E-mail within 24 to 48 hours.
Regularly taking four or five days to get back to coworkers tarnish-
es your image.

> **Stay organized.** Losing correspondence or fumbling around for
reports buried in a two-foot-high stack of paper gives the impression that everything you do is equally inefficient.

> **Do what you say you will do.** This is so obvious it hardly seems nec-
essary to mention. However, it is far too common for employees to
break their word on what they consider small things. When it comes
to your reputation, there are no small things. In fact, small things
often attract much attention. If you say you will call tomorrow, call

tomorrow. If you say you will mail it today, mail it today. If you say you will be there at three o'clock, be there at three o'clock. Doing small things well suggests that everything you do will be done well. Consistently slipping up on little things makes coworkers and bosses suspicious that everything you do is slipshod.

> **Volunteer.** If a coworker is struggling with software you know well, share your knowledge. Lending a helping hand lets everyone, including bosses, know you're a team player, and they will want you on their team. Chipping in also helps you network with others throughout the organization. Of course, doing favors for others makes it much easier to ask for favors in return.

Wherever man goes to dwell, his character goes with him.
—AFRICAN PROVERB

< *Body Language* >

He looked at me like I was a dish he hadn't ordered.
—RING LARDNER

Other people tend to form their opinion of us rather quickly. They size us up by the clothes we wear and the language we use. They also use our gestures, expressions, and the way we carry ourselves to decide what kind of person we are. Some experts believe that nonverbal communication may be even more important than our words. Here's how to use body language to project the image of a confident and competent person:

> Eye contact. We tend to respect those who feel comfortable looking us directly in the eye. We also take it as a signal of a confident, open, and honest person. Those who avoid eye contact are often perceived as shy or unsure of themselves. Sometimes it can be interpreted as a sign of untruthfulness. **Make eye contact, but avoid staring.** We feel uncomfortable when someone looks directly at us for longer than a few seconds. Alternate looking into a person's eyes and looking away.

> Facial expressions. **Facial expressions reinforce the verbal messages we send.** A poker face makes it more difficult for others to read and understand our messages. Using smiles, frowns, and other facial expressions can help convey your message.

> Natural gestures. Act as naturally and freely as circumstances allow.

Smile, nod your head in agreement, make eye contact, and use facial and hand gestures to help make your point.

> Speaking with a soft or hesitant voice can be interpreted as a sign of insecurity. **Aim for a firm yet relaxed and friendly tone.** Avoid a monotone. Try to eliminate verbal habits like "you know," "um," and "uh."

> Standing. **Another way to appear confident and professional is to stand up straight, in a natural way.** Leaning against walls, standing with stooped shoulders, and having a fidgety or rigid stance can be distracting to those you're talking to.

> Walking. **Moving from place to place with a healthy stride, head up, and arms swinging freely conveys self-assurance.** It indicates that you know where you are going and are eager to get there. Short strides, dragging feet, and a slow pace create the opposite impression.

> Distance. Depending on the circumstances, people may feel uncomfortable when others stand too close. **When conversing, respect a coworker's personal space** by standing about three feet from them. If the other person appears uncomfortable or slowly backs away from you, it may be because you are standing too close.

> Mannerisms. Finger-drumming, humming, cracking gum, mumbling, clicking a pen, and other forms of fidgeting can be distracting to coworkers. Such habits may indicate stress or boredom. Work at controlling them. Replacing them with a more constructive habit sometimes helps.

> Touching. Some people are open and expressive. Touching others in conversation is natural for them. However, some people do not like to be touched. **Be cautious about touching others, especially members of the opposite sex.** It could be taken the wrong way. Touching bosses is sometimes seen as being too familiar.

Nothing is more revealing than movement.
—MARTHA GRAHAM

< *Jargon* >

The limits of my language are the limits of my world.
—LUDWIG WITTGENSTEIN

Jargon is a collection of special words, expressions, and acronyms used within industries, professions, and companies. Acronyms are formed with the first letters of several words of a term. For instance, TD for touchdown, ETA for estimated time of arrival, and DRG for diagnosis-related group. Professionals and people working in an industry rely heavily on jargon because it saves time talking to one another. **The faster you pick up the language of your work, the faster you'll be able to understand and contribute to work conversations.** Using jargon also indicates a knowledge and interest in your industry and company. **Here's how to learn your new language:**

> **Ask.** If a coworker uses a term you don't understand, ask for an explanation. However, don't become a nuisance by interrupting every time you hear a new word.

> **Listen.** Jot down acronyms and terms you don't understand. Find their meaning before you use them incorrectly.

> **Read.** Trade and professional publications are a great way to keep up with developments in your field. Borrow back issues from a co-worker, company library, or public library. Also look for books dedicated to defining terms used in your industry and profession.

> **Be careful. There are no standard rules.** Sometimes acronyms are

pronounced as one word. DOS (rhymes with boss), for disk oper-
ating system, is an example. But sometimes the individual letters
are pronounced. For instance, the acronym for an electrocardio-
gram is pronouncd by saying the letters ECG. Pronouncing the letters DOS instead of saying one word indicates that you're a rook-
ie. So be sure of pronunciations and meanings before using jargon.

> **Be considerate.** Jargon is used to communicate quickly and effec-
tively. **When talking to those outside your industry or profession,
it's best to avoid jargon** for several reasons. First, your listener
probably won't understand what you say. Second, using jargon
among the uninitiated irritates more than it impresses.

When ideas fail, words come in very handy.
—GOETHE

< *Priorities* >

There is nothing so useless as doing efficiently
that which should not be done at all.
—PETER F. DRUCKER

Employees generally have more work to do than time permits. There may be short-term exceptions, but eventually, the situation is adjusted with more work or fewer employees. Such workload pressures require employees to set priorities. They must decide which tasks are the most important and accomplish them first. Here are some tips on setting your own priorities:

> **Align priorities.** Understand the priorities of your company, department, and boss. Keep them in mind when deciding how to spend your time or which project to tackle first. Working hard is not enough. Make sure you concentrate on the projects your employer considers important.

> **Beware of perfection.** Don't try to do everything perfectly. Designing an elaborate cover for an internal report for your boss can take up valuable time. Ask yourself if a task is worth the time you're spending on it. Be honest. If it isn't, move on to something more meaningful.

> **Don't fall prey to interruptions.** If you're working on something important and a coworker wants to chitchat, ask for a rain check. If someone asks for a few minutes' help on something minor, suggest another time. Interruptions will cause you to lose

momentum. Besides, a "few minutes' help" has a way of turning into a few hours.

> **Beware of rituals.** It's easy to slip into workplace rituals, such as starting the day by arranging your desk, reading a business magazine, or exploring software features. Be wary of time wasters that give the illusion of getting something done.

> **Plan.** Start the day with a plan focused on the most important tasks. Set goals and deadlines. Use the time-honored technique of making lists to help stay on track.

> **Learn to say no.** It's foolhardy to take on more than you can realistically handle. Don't volunteer to run errands or cover for a sick employee if it means putting off more important work.

> **Reflect.** Periodically look up from the hectic pace of everyday work. Are you putting life's really important things first? Are you nurturing relationships with family and friends? Are you using your natural talents? Are you looking after your physical and emotional health? Are you growing personally and professionally?

We are confronted with insurmountable opportunities.
—POGO (WALT KELLY)

< *Details* >

It's a poor sort of memory that only works backwards.
—LEWIS CARROLL

It doesn't take many slipups to earn the reputation for being disorganized. So it's important to have a way to keep track of appointments, tasks, deadlines, and meetings.

Written reminders remove the stress of trying to remember everything. And they help alleviate nagging doubts that you may have forgotten something important. Experiment with ways to keep track of details so you can free your mind for more creative pursuits. Here are a few tips on paying attention to the details:

> **As soon as you're asked to do something or be somewhere at a given time, write it down.** Include the date, time, location, and other pertinent facts. Desk and pocket calendars are popular tools. Electronic personal information managers are also helpful.

> **If you use a calendar, write in pencil** so you can easily revise entries.

> **Start each day by reviewing the day's activities.** If something comes up and you're unable to make an appointment, notify those involved as soon as possible.

> **End each day by looking at the next day's entries.** That way you'll be prepared for the early morning meeting.

> **Keep "to do" lists.** One way is to write tasks on three-by-five-inch slips of paper. Store them by the phone so you can review them while you're on hold or listening to your voice mail. When a task has been completed, throw away the reminder.

God is in the details.
—UNKNOWN

< *Habit* >

The nature of men is always the same;
it is their habits that separate them.
—CONFUCIUS

Most of us have two vocabularies: words we understand when we hear or read them, and a much smaller vocabulary of words we use when speaking. We fall into the habit of using the same words over and over, and they become our verbal repertoire. The same is true of the skills presented in this book. It is one thing to "know" them. It is another thing entirely to use skills often enough so that they become habitual. Here are some tips on developing good workplace habits:

> **Understand the power of habit.** Anything we repeatedly do becomes habitual. Watching television, sleeping late, driving fast, and exercising regularly are good examples. Sheer habit also has a lot to do with whether we're courteous or discourteous, patient or impatient, optimistic or pessimistic.

> **Start early.** As every golfer knows, once a bad habit is established, it is difficult to replace it with a good one. Early in your career, do things the preferred way so you develop good work skills—not bad ones that need to be replaced.

> **Do just-in-time reviews.** Shortly before you're scheduled to be given a task or hold a meeting, review the principles presented in this book.

> **Critique your performance.** Compare your performance with the approach suggested by this resource. Note your weaknesses, and jot down ways to improve.

> **Seek advice.** Ask others how you can improve your performance. Use specific questions, like "How could the opening of my presentation have been improved?" or "How could I have done a better job of keeping the meeting on track?"

> **Be systematic.** Periodically choose a skill to concentrate on. Read about the skill, and practice it. Observe how others perform. Do that for a month, and then move on to another skill. If we ignore the power of habit, it's sure to work against us. Investing in worthwhile habits will pay lifelong dividends.

It seems, in fact, as though the second half of a man's life is made up of nothing but the habits he has accumulated in the first half.
—FYODOR DOSTOYEVSKY

< *Blowing Your Own Horn* >

Don't be too humble, you're not that great.
—GOLDA MEIR

Bosses are busy people with much on their minds. It's quite possible that your fine work and extra efforts will go unnoticed by a preoccupied boss. You must blow your own horn. That means you make sure others, especially your bosses, know about your hard work, initiative, and successes. Here are some tips:

> **Don't overdo it.** If you draw attention to yourself too often, it will look like you're bragging. Boasting usually isn't well received by bosses or coworkers.

> **Be subtle.** Talk about yourself indirectly. Instead of saying, "I thought you should know I helped Mary with that urgent project," say "Mary is going to take me to lunch today to thank me for helping her with the big project." Instead of "I was very busy while you were on vacation," say "I reorganized the files last week and found the contract you thought you had lost."

> **Be selective.** Blow your horn for major accomplishments. Your boss may question your priorities if you proudly announce you completed a small or routine task. After all, it is your job. Drop hints about efforts or successes that go beyond the call of duty or require special skills. It's one thing to back up the computer files. It's another to write a program to do it automatically.

> **Be creative.** Use variety in your public-relations campaign so you'll avoid the appearance of bragging or buttering up the boss. A written "progress report" may be effective under some circumstances. Telling a humorous story about something that happened while you were working late may be entertaining and get your message across at the same time.

It pays to advertise.
—Unknown

< *Embarrassment* >

Nobody can make you feel inferior without your consent.
—ELEANOR ROOSEVELT

Working with other people means awkward and embarrassing situations will occasionally occur. Handling them with confidence and ease helps everyone get through these uncomfortable moments. **How you react to a difficult situation can turn an awkward moment to your advantage.** Here are some reminders:

When it happens to others:

> **Don't laugh.** Laughing at another's embarrassment is a sure way to lose respect.

> **Look the other way.** If you see someone dip his tie into his soup, look away. Help the victim feel less uncomfortable by allowing them to think there were no witnesses.

> **Be matter-of-fact.** If someone at lunch has spaghetti sauce in his mustache or spinach in her teeth, be matter-of-fact. A simple "You have something in your mustache" quickly followed by conversation will make everyone at the table feel more comfortable.

> **Top it.** If someone spills an entire cup of coffee on the conference-room table, help make light of it while the cleanup goes on. Mention an amusing story about the times you did a similar or even more embarrassing thing.

> **Get help.** You may notice a member of the opposite sex with torn clothing or a zipper that needs zipping. If you can't find the right time or words to alert the person, mention the situation to a friend or colleague, who will be glad to help out.

> **Downplay it.** If someone calls you by the wrong name, spills something on you, or damages one of your possessions, stay calm. Use a ready phrase, like "Think nothing of it" or "Please don't give it another thought."

When it happens to you:

> **Remain calm.** Embarrassment is contagious. If you're flustered or agitated, others will feel uncomfortable, too. Act as if what you've done is hardly worth noticing, and confidently proceed through the awkward moment. Of course, do apologize if appropriate.

> **Use humor.** If the situation permits and you can think of something funny, say it. Poking a little fun at ourselves shows we haven't over-reacted. It also gives us a chance to display a healthy sense of humor.

I've only met four perfect people in my life
and I didn't like any of them.
—UNKNOWN

< *Procrastination* >

This is the earliest I've ever been late.
—YOGI BERRA

Most of us put off doing small tasks that aren't challenging, interesting, or gratifying. Some of us also have a difficult time starting major projects—even if they are important to our success on the job. Sometimes we procrastinate because we predict a task will be too hard, take too long, or won't be worth the effort. Or, we may fear failure. We worry and fret instead of getting started. **Here are some tips on how to break this self-defeating tendency:**

> **Think action.** It's easy to procrastinate when hard work is at hand and rewards are far off. Look beyond the effort of getting started. Instead, focus on how happy and successful you'll feel when the work is done.

> **Act quickly.** The longer we think about getting started, the more likely we are to come up with reasons not to. Weighing the pros and cons over and over does little good. Just get started.

> **Don't look too far ahead.** Projects, such as recommending a new work process to your boss (and changing careers), often never go beyond the planning stage. Anticipating how you'll handle every detail or make every decision can paralyze you. Writers don't wait until every comma is mentally in place before they begin writing. They rely on the very act of writing to bring forth ideas and solutions. Once you're under way,

you'll be able to concentrate on obstacles one at a time—as they surface.

> **Gain momentum.** Major tasks often involve many sessions, and each session means starting from scratch. Writers are noted for devising tricks to help ease themselves into action. One famous author uses a ritual of sharpening several pencils to help him get started. Another ends her writing in the middle of a sentence to make the next session easier to start. Try similar techniques to prime the pump.

> **Don't confuse motion for progress.** Cleaning up computer files, ordering supplies, and doing "research" can feel like progress, when in fact they may be delay tactics. Tackling a difficult piece of the project first is a good way to get your energy, enthusiasm, and confidence flowing.

> **Be decisive.** Fretting over postponed tasks is more tiring than the tasks themselves. Accept that you'll sometimes lack the energy, concentration, or initiative to take on some jobs. To help from feeling guilty, don't postpone the job indefinitely. Set a specific time, such as the following day, when you'll reconsider. Until then, work on other things and enjoy a clear conscience.

Even if you're on the right track,
you'll get run over if you just sit there.
—WILL ROGERS

< Shortcuts >

We must use time as a tool not as a couch.
—John F. Kennedy

Many workplaces have a hectic pace. It seems that every task is important and must be finished right away. **No doubt, you'll be tempted to try shortcuts. But you can easily get caught up in a pattern of "do it fast, do it wrong, do it again."** Oddly enough, rework becomes so common that we often confuse it with progress.

Here are some ideas on getting the job done well, on time, and with minimum stress:

> **Understand the purpose. Ask questions!** Go beyond knowing what needs to be done. Make sure you know why. Understand how your project fits into the larger picture. Then it's easier to make decisions, recommendations, and improvements.

> **Plan.** Resist the temptation to jump right in and get started. What you perceive as quick progress can turn into running around in circles. There is no substitute for a well-thought-out plan. This is true for any size project.

> **Develop a timetable.** Estimate how long each step will take. But keep in mind that things usually take longer than expected. Be conservative, and allow adequate time to recover from inevitable slipups.

> **Identify key assumptions.** Periodically review and challenge factors you take for granted. Is it safe to assume the parts are in stock? Is

it wise to assume staffing will be at 100 percent for the duration of the project? Develop contingency plans.

> **Communicate.** As soon as possible, alert everyone who will be involved in the project or affected by it. Written communication is best. This is the time to find out about vacation plans and other schedules that may impact your strategy. You don't want to discover at the last minute that key helpers will be on vacation just when you need them most.

> **Delegate.** If you have the opportunity, spread the work around. Trying to do everything yourself is often counterproductive. Use the talents and skills of those who have proven track records. Let them do the work they are good at.

> **Stay in touch.** Routinely contact helpers to make sure everything is going well. Understand their plans, and follow their progress so you'll be sure there are no misunderstandings. Stay on top of matters.

> **Check your work.** Don't send out a report without carefully reading it and checking all the math. By all means, ask someone else to review it as well. Remember, even simple errors, like misspellings or omitted pages, cast a shadow of doubt on your credibility.

> **Share the glory.** If things go well, thank everyone who helped. If things could have gone better, take responsibility. Don't make excuses or blame your staff. Learn from the experience so the next project goes better.

I am long on ideas but short on time.
—THOMAS A. EDISON

< *Mistakes* >

Experience is the name everyone gives to their mistakes.
—OSCAR WILDE

Mistakes are an inevitable part of every human endeavor. Your working life will be sprinkled with them. They may range from forgetting a meeting to launching a product that flops, from graphing the wrong data to purchasing the wrong-sized parts, from misspelling a client's name to making bad investments. **Big and little, you'll make them. Here's how to react to mistakes:**

> **Step forward right away.** Resist the temptation to remain silent and hope no one notices and nothing bad happens. Sooner or later, mistakes surface. The longer you postpone admission, the longer the mistake has to snowball into something larger, with unpredictable results. And, in the long run, saying nothing and praying that all goes well is more stressful than owning up.

> **Keep your composure.** Admit the mistake, using the right combination of poise, confidence, and self-assurance. The way you handle the situation may say more about you than the mistake itself. State the facts, for example: "I sent the package to the wrong client."

> **Don't offer excuses.** The deed is done, and no litany of excuses is needed or helpful. Saying "I was busy" or "I thought Tom took care of that" or "I told Mary to do it yesterday" sounds like you're denying responsibility or passing the buck.

> **Suggest damage control.** After owning up, suggest solutions or inform your boss of actions you've already taken. For instance, say, "I suggest we call the clients and tell them we'll ship new proposals tomorrow."

> **Volunteer.** Since you caused the difficulties, help correct them. "I'll stay tonight and prepare new proposals" prevents your mistake from becoming your boss' problem.

> **Learn from this experience.** Look for the fundamental reason for the mistake. Were you tired from a late night out? Were you rushing matters? Did you forget to follow up with a coworker? Should you have delegated parts of the project? Did you try a shortcut? Mistakes are understandable; recurring mistakes are not.

> **Don't be too hard on yourself.** Dwelling on and talking about the mistake isn't fruitful. Don't make a big deal out of it, but do use the experience to avoid future mistakes.

A life making mistakes is not only more honorable
but more useful than a life spent doing nothing.
—GEORGE BERNARD SHAW

< *Money* >

I'd like to live like a poor man with lots of money.
—PABLO PICASSO

The optimism and energy of youth make it difficult to imagine rainy days and old age. But the best time to think about them and start saving for those rainy days is the first day of your first real job. Here's why:

> **Jobs are not guaranteed.** At one time, workers counted on job security. They assumed an uninterrupted string of paychecks from the same employer until their retirement. **Today, it's prudent to plan on at least one spell of unemployment and to save up money for a nest egg to get you through it.**

> **Health care is expensive.** Health insurance is a very important and valuable fringe benefit. If you lose your job, your employer will probably be required by law to allow you to purchase health insurance from the plan you were enrolled in. However, the cost is likely to be much higher than the amount you had been paying while employed. A nest egg ensures you'll be able to pay for health insurance.

> **Money is expensive.** The interest rate charged on bank loans and credit-card balances is steep. A nest egg means you won't need to borrow money at high rates if you lose your job.

> Laws change. **It's risky to assume that Social Security will be available in its current form when you retire.** For instance, there is talk

of changing the retirement age to 70. Without a nest egg, you won't determine your retirement age—the government will.

> **Education is expensive.** Many people use unemployment as an opportunity to change careers. This sometimes requires additional education or training. A nest egg affords you the chance to switch careers and land the job of your dreams.

> **Opportunities require money.** A nest egg may enable you to take advantage of sudden opportunities, such as buying a house or business.

> Compound interest is powerful. **The sooner a savings plan is started, the more impressive the results.** For example, saving $50 a month from age 25 to age 65 will grow to about $316,000 at 10 percent interest. If you wait until age 35 to start, your nest egg will total only $113,000.

> **Employers can help.** You're not on your own in setting up a nest egg. Many employers offer valuable assistance with profit-sharing plans and tax-deferred annuities. Some offer financial-planning services. Understand your options, and get help making good decisions.

I've been rich and I've been poor; rich is better.
—SOPHIE TUCKER

< *Computers* >

In the computer world, hardware is anything you can hit
with a hammer, software is what you can only curse at.

—UNKNOWN

Personal computers have quickly become the all-purpose office tool. Secretaries, receiving clerks, salespeople, accounting clerks, and managers use them. **Employers value employees who are "computer literate"** and know how to put computers to good use.

Here's a computer primer:

> Hardware refers to equipment such as the computer, monitor, printer, and other attachments. Software refers to the programs used by the computer to perform tasks.

> Computers come in many sizes. They include mainframe, mini, personal or desktop, laptop, and notebook. Mainframe and mini computers are the most powerful, and they are usually located in the data processing department. Workers access them via a terminal or smaller computer linked to them by cable. Laptop and notebook computers are portable and can be carried by salespeople when they call on customers. Personal or desktop computers usually remain at a workstation.

> There are many software categories. Word processing, spreadsheet, database, and desktop-publishing software are the most common. **Word processing programs are used for writing letters, memos, and reports. Spreadsheets perform math functions** on financial and

other data. **Database software is used to store large amounts of data** such as names, addresses, and other information about customers. **Desktop-publishing software is used for newsletters and booklets**—material that often requires graphics. Most software is versatile and is used for many purposes beyond these few examples.

> **Data are commonly stored on individual personal computers.** That means information stored on one computer is not readily accessible by other computer users. **To remedy that, personal computers are "networked." They are connected to one another by cable so that data on one machine can be accessed by other workers on their computers.** Networking also permits the use of electronic mail, often called E-mail. Security measures limit access to data and mail.

> **It's possible to use telephone lines to retrieve information stored on computers throughout the world via hardware called a modem.** Many people access computer bulletin boards and on-line services from home. They keep current on sports, news, and Wall Street. They also play games, send messages, and "chat" with other users. It is also possible to access the card catalogs of public and college libraries throughout the world. Employers also permit employees to connect to the company computer from home and while traveling.

> Computers are becoming ever more powerful, versatile, and popular. However, one thing has remained fairly constant: to use them efficiently, it helps to know touch-typing. **If you don't know how to type, learn.** Software is available to help you learn quickly and easily.

I do not fear computers. I fear the lack of them.
—Isaac Asimov

< *E-mail* >

Language is a form of organized stutter.
—MARSHALL McLUHAN

Electronic mail, or E-mail as it is commonly called, is used in most large organizations. It's an efficient way to send messages and other information from one computer to another.

First, a word of caution. **Assume that your E-mail is not private.** Your employer can easily monitor your mail. In addition, it is much too easy to accidentally send messages to the wrong people. Jobs have been lost this way.

What follows is an E-mail primer. Your employer's system may include fewer or more features than these:

> **Employees are assigned electronic mailboxes. Passwords are used to secure them.** Sending a message can be as easy as typing it, choosing the recipient's name from a list, and clicking a "Send" button.

> **Messages can be sent to numerous recipients simultaneously. The recipients could be located anywhere in the building or anywhere in the world** if your employer provides that kind of E-mail system.

> **Unlike conventional paper-based mail, E-mail usually takes seconds or minutes to arrive at its destination.** A sound or icon on the user's screen usually alerts employees that E-mail has arrived. E-mail can easily be printed.

> **It's possible to attach computer files to E-mail.** Suppose you've written a report on your word processor and you want to share it with the home office. No need to retype it as E-mail. You can send the report's file as an electronic attachment to your message.

> **It's possible to forward messages.** If you receive a message of interest to others, you can forward it to them. However, you should get permission from the sender before you forward their message, especially if it is potentially controversial or private.

> **It's possible to broadcast your message.** If you routinely send messages to the same group of coworkers, you can establish a mail group. A single click of the mouse will send the message to everyone in the group. Be careful. Clicking on the wrong group could send confidential information to the wrong people.

> **You can allow others to read your mail.** For instance, a secretary may have permission to view the boss' mail. However, mail can be sent confidentially in order to prevent proxy users from seeing it.

> **You can reply automatically.** If you are on vacation, you probably want those who send you mail to know that. It's possible to have your computer automatically reply to each person who sends you a message while you are gone. You will still receive mail, and it may even be possible to check your mail from home or from the beach.

> **Be considerate. Because it is almost effortless to send E-mail, it's easy to overdo it.** Limit the number of "carbon" copies you send so you don't interrupt coworkers with messages that don't interest or concern them. Also, send thank-you notes only for significant favors.

> Check your spelling and punctuation. Assume that your message will be printed, so take the same precautions you would with paper correspondence.

> **Be security conscious.** If you leave your computer on and your mailbox open, others may be able to read your mail. Worse, they may be able to send mail that looks as if it came from you.

> **Clean house. Routinely delete old messages from your mailbox.** This saves space on the company's computer. Remember, even though you delete messages, your company may maintain copies of them without your knowledge.

Progress might have been all right once, but it's gone on too long.
—OGDEN NASH

< *The Internet* >

Any sufficiently advanced technology is indistinguishable from magic.
—ARTHUR C. CLARKE

Employers are increasingly giving their employees access to the Internet. In addition, the Internet and the World Wide Web are popular topics of conversational.

First, a word of caution. The Internet provides access to all kinds of words, conversations, software, sounds, and pictures. Much of it is business related, but much of it is not. **Be aware that your employer may keep track of not only how often you use the Internet, but which sites you visit.**

Here's an Internet primer:

> **The U.S. Department of Defense created the Internet about 25 years ago. However, no one owns or controls it.** Until about five or six years ago, the Internet was relatively unknown outside scientific and technical communities.

> **Simply stated, the Internet comprises millions of computers connected to one another via telephone lines and similar means. The World Wide Web is one part of the Internet** that is easy to use, includes "pages" filled with text and colorful pictures, and is growing rapidly.

> **The Internet and the World Wide Web have two primary uses: to communicate and share information.** Communication is done via

E-mail. Information is shared primarily by users reading one another's pages. Information can also be shared by sending files from one computer to another.

> Connecting to the Internet from home is usually done via telephone lines. **Users need an account with an Internet Service Provider (ISP).** Rate schedules include a fixed fee per month for unlimited usage, hourly charges, or a combination.

> **Users find their way to pages in two ways. First, they type the Internet address of the site they want to visit.** Such addresses are often advertised in magazines, on television, in newspapers, on radio, and on billboards. **Second, addresses can be found by using search engines that are available for free on the Internet. Search engines are easy-to-use programs that find sites related to key words typed by the user.** For instance, a list of thousands of sites can be generated by simply typing the word "computer."

> Images, sounds, and radio programs are also available on the Internet. It's truly a window on the world.

The past went that-a-way.
—MARSHALL McLUHAN

SOCIAL SKILLS

< Office Attire >

Clothes make the man;
naked people have little or no influence in society.
—MARK TWAIN

How we dress in our country has changed considerably in the last twenty years. We've loosened up, and parts of the business world have as well.** For instance, some companies permit casual attire. Others relax dress codes on designated days. **Despite these changes, personal appearance is still important in the workplace.** Employees can jeopardize their careers by assuming otherwise.

You may think it unfair, but employers, bosses, coworkers, and customers make sweeping assumptions about us based on our outward appearances. Keep in mind:

> Use toothpaste, mouthwash, and deodorant. Keep fingernails trimmed and hands clean.

> Body hair should be clean and neatly trimmed.

> Keep your shoes on—even if your feet are hidden under your desk.

> If your company has a written dress code, follow it. If not, observe how your boss, other managers, and savvy coworkers dress. **You will**

be expected to adopt the company style through observation and imitation. Different industries and professions have different unwritten rules of dress.

> Keep your wardrobe clean, pressed, and odor free. Buy good shoes, keep them polished, and replace worn heels.

> Don't wear revealing, provocative, or outright sexy clothing.

> **Even if in-office attire is casual, dress up if you expect to meet outsiders or otherwise represent the company.**

> **Remember that perfumes, colognes, and aftershaves can be distracting and even offensive. Be conservative**—only those standing very near you should be aware of the fragrance. Consider asking those working near you if you're in the habit of overdoing it.

> If you attend a meeting or function outside the office and someone is inappropriately dressed, ignore it and say nothing. A compliment is the only time it is appropriate to mention someone else's appearance.

Fashions fade, style is eternal.
—YVES SAINT LAURENT

< *Meeting People* >

I never knew a man I didn't like.
—WILL ROGERS

Being at ease and putting others at ease when you meet or introduce strangers is a mark of a well-mannered person. Here are some ways to make good introductions and a good first impression:

Being introduced:

> **Smile and look directly at the person you are being introduced to.** A simple "Hello," "How do you do?" or "It's nice to meet you" works just fine.

> Be ready to rescue the person making the introductions in case they forget your name. If they do, simply extend your hand and say, "Hello, I'm Scott Francis."

> **Repeating the name of the person you just met helps you remember it.** "Mr. Jones, I hope you enjoy your visit," adds a personal touch as well.

> If no one is available to make the introduction, extend your hand and introduce yourself with something like "Hello, I'm Scott Francis from the marketing department."

Making introductions:

> The simplest introduction is simply "Ms. Keefer—Mr. Eilers." **Avoid using first names only, unless your workplace is a casual one.**

> If, for the life of you, you can't remember a person's name, make a half-introduction: "Have you met Mr. Carpenter?" The unnamed person should complete the introduction with "I'm Al Eilers. How do you do?" If they do not, let it go at that.

> **After some introductions, an icebreaker may be appropriate.** In a social setting, you may want to say something like "Jose Morales, this is Al Eilers. Al just bought a personal computer, too." Mention something that is light and not controversial. In a business setting, say something like "Alice Jones, this is Nancy Burger. Nancy was recently transferred from the marketing department in our Michigan office."

I am a person. Do not bend, fold, spindle or mutilate.
—Picket sign at the Berkeley riots, 1964

< *Shaking Hands* >

*It has long been an axiom of mine
that the little things are infinitely the most important.*
—Sir Arthur Conan Doyle

Knowing when and how to shake hands is an important part of making a good impression. It's a sign of professionalism, poise, and confidence. At one time, women waited for men to extend their hands to them. The current practice is for men and women to extend their hands to one another. Some tips:

How to shake hands:

> Smile and present your right hand in a warm and enthusiastic motion. **Extend your hand in a decisive way.** Don't be hesitant or give the impression that you're unsure of what to do or say.

> Look at the other person's hand to make sure you'll grasp it. (You don't want to miss and act out a Laurel and Hardy routine!) **Grasp the other person's entire hand.** Grabbing a handful of fingers leaves a poor impression.

> Look the person in the eyes.

> **Use a firm, not a bone-crushing or wimpy (dead fish) grip.** Two or three shakes are sufficient. Let go, and withdraw your hand.

Shake hands when you:

> are introduced to someone;

> call on a customer (and when you depart);

> are visited by someone outside your company (and when they depart);

> by chance meet someone you know on the street, in a restaurant, or in some other public place. Shake hands again on departing;

> congratulate someone at an awards, retirement, or similar function.

Miscellaneous:

> If you are at a social or business gathering in which it may be necessary to frequently shake hands, keep your right hand free. Consider holding your drink or papers in your left hand.

> Do not extend your hand to someone who cannot return the handshake. Examples are those who have an armload of packages or those with a disability.

> If your extended hand is not seen or acknowledged, simply draw it back. It's awkward, but it happens. Don't take offense.

You cannot shake hands with a clenched fist.
—INDIRA GANDHI

< *Small Talk* >

Talking about your troubles is no good.
Eighty percent of your friends don't care and the rest are glad.
—TOMMY LASORDA

Small talk is common in the business world. Salespeople rely on it when calling on customers. It's used to break the ice while people wait for a meeting to start. It's made when employees wait for an elevator or find themselves in the photocopying room with a member of executive management. Your image will suffer if you're prone to awkward exchanges or uncomfortable silences. It will be enhanced if you can easily chat with people at all levels in the organization. **Here are tips on making small talk:**

> **Understand its purpose.** It isn't done to say something profound or terribly interesting. **Sometimes it's a way to feel comfortable with another person before the real business is discussed.** In other cases, such as waiting for an elevator, small talk acknowledges the presence of another human being. **Sometimes it signals that you are a warm, friendly person who is interested in other people.**

> **You may want to have a cursory knowledge of what's happening in the world of sports, which many people like to discuss.** Even if you are not a sports fan, it helps to read over the front page of the sports section. That way you can at least join in small talk about a recent game or event.

> **Be informed.** Some current events are good small-talk topics. It helps to know that the president of the United States will visit your city the following day or that a major earthquake hit California yesterday. Knowing about current events gives you topics for small talk. Ignorance of major local and world events can be embarrassing.

> **Pick neutral topics.** Aim for a brief, friendly, and upbeat exchange.

> **Use discretion.** In this age of sexual harassment, it's possible to be perceived as being too friendly. If someone does not warmly respond to your banter, don't persist. You may be coming off the wrong way or they may be misinterpreting your motive.

> **Be ready.** Successful exchanges of small talk with company leaders as you ride the elevator can't hurt your career. Be ready to confidently bring up and chat about a recent company television commercial or similar business event. Display your interest in your company's business. Make a good impression.

It is completely unimportant.
That is why it is so interesting.
—AGATHA CHRISTIE

< *Conversation* >

Nature has given us two ears but only one mouth.
—BENJAMIN DISRAELI

Those we consider good at conversation are actually good at listening and helping others participate. Sometimes people who actually say little are considered good conversationalists and are a welcome addition to any group. They probably use some of these techniques:

> **Take the initiative.** Be the first to say hello, then follow up with a ready icebreaker. Friendly comments or questions about the weather, sports, or room you're in are favorite topics. Your purpose isn't to be profound—it's to let others know you're friendly and willing to talk. You could remark on the color scheme used in the room, the view outside the window, or something that happened on your way there.

> **Move the conversation along. Give lots of feedback when the other person speaks. Use verbal signals like "mm-hmm" and "yes."** A nod, smile, or eye contact lets the speaker know you're interested.

> **Don't monopolize the conversation.** Let the other person do at least half of the talking. Encourage others to continue their remarks by using open-ended questions, like "How did you feel?" or "Then what happened?"

> **Be upbeat.** Avoid bringing up unpleasant topics, like personal problems or illnesses. Whiners, complainers, and hypochondriacs can be bores!

> **Don't ask about personal matters,** such as income, religion, race, age, politics, weight, physical handicaps, or the cost of cars, clothes, or jewelry.

> **Limit interruptions.** Some will happen by accident, of course. Take your turn when others look to you. Pause when you see someone else is ready to speak so they may take a turn.

> **Don't try to impress others.** People quickly see through name-droppers. And those who manage to slip in references to expensive possessions, vacations, and colleges aren't considered genuine.

> **Don't tell off-color, sexist, or racist jokes.** If you have any doubt about how a comment will be taken, keep it to yourself.

> **Avoid politics and religion.** Reserve these topics for discussions with close friends.

> **Don't top someone's story.** If your vacation was more exotic, describe it later. Let the speaker enjoy the attention, and don't steal their thunder.

> **Don't correct anyone else's grammar.** A slip of the tongue or ignorance may be the cause. In either case, let it pass. Listen to what is meant, not what is said.

> **Don't challenge minor "factual" errors.** If it really doesn't matter if the score was five to four and not three to two, let it ride. If you must dispute a fact, do it graciously with a comment like "Oh, I thought…"

> **Draw others into the conversation.** A shy person will probably appreciate it when you include them with an easy, open-ended question, like "What do you like most about your job?"

> **Know when to change topics or end the conversation.** People often let us know when they want to end the discussion. Look for sighs, restlessness, diminished eye contact, and steps backward. These indicate it's time to graciously wrap it up and move on. In large gatherings, after about ten minutes, it's often time to move to another group. However, be cautious about approaching two people who seem to be involved in an intense conversation. They may not want to be interrupted.

A single conversation across the table with a wise man
is worth a month's study of books.
—CHINESE PROVERB

< *Disabilities* >

All the bountiful sentiments in the world
weigh less than a single lovely action.
—JAMES RUSSELL LOWELL

Many of us feel awkward in the presence of those with disabilities. We'd like to be of help, but we're not sure if help is wanted. We're often afraid of doing the wrong thing, so we don't offer assistance when it may be welcomed. Here are some things to consider:

> **Jumping in with unwanted assistance is as bad as doing nothing.**

> If you see a disabled person in a situation—such as a person in a wheelchair navigating a long hill—simply ask, "Would you like help?" Ask in the same way you would ask anyone who was struggling with an armful of packages. **If the disabled person wants help, he will say so.** If help isn't required, he will appreciate the offer nonetheless. This simple question eliminates potential embarrassment and awkwardness.

> It is impolite to ask about a disability. "What happened to your legs?" is an inappropriate question. Allow the disabled person to share such personal information if and when they prefer.

It's coexistence or no existence.
—BERTRAND RUSSELL

< *Apologizing* >

Eating words has never given me indigestion.
—Winston Churchill

We interact with many people in innumerable situations while at work. Now and then, all of us accidentally create an awkward or embarrassing situation. We may use language that comes out stronger than we wanted. In an unthinking moment we may inadvertently hurt someone's feelings. Here's how to apologize:

> **Accept that awkward situations happen to everyone.** Don't fret or berate yourself—simply make amends.

> Don't allow too much time to pass between the "hurt" and your apology.

> **Find a time and place to speak in private.** Apologies are uncomfortable for both parties. No audience is necessary.

> **Do not try to disown the error by making excuses.** You are seeking forgiveness not sympathy. A sincere "Please forgive me" is a good way to start.

> **Keep in mind that you may be rebuffed.** If this happens, you've done your part. The responsibility for mending the relationship passes to the other person. Give it time. It often takes a while for injured feelings to heal. Sometimes it is as hard to accept an apology

as it is to make one. After you've made your gesture, go on with your relationship as if nothing had happened.

> **Learn something.** Reflect on what caused the initial situation and your poor reaction. Plan ways to avoid it in the future.

> If you lose or damage someone's possession, apologize and do the best you can to have it fixed or replaced.

I do not want people to be agreeable,
as it saves me the trouble of liking them.
—JANE AUSTEN

< *Questions* >

If you had listened hard enough,
you might have heard what I meant to say.
—ROD McKUEN

Questions are used for much more than simply obtaining information.
Here are a few examples:

> Your boss walks in and asks, "Do you think it's time these keyboards were cleaned?"

> Your coworker asks, "I just finished this report cover. How does it look to you?"

> At a party, your spouse asks, "What time is it?"

> A member of your lunch group asks, "Do you think I should use my vacation to go to Japan or England?"

These are questions all right, but they are not simple requests for information. **The motive must be understood in order to correctly respond.**

> Your boss is really saying "Please clean the keyboards." She is probably not interested in knowing that the keyboards were cleaned two weeks ago. The message is: clean them.

> The coworker who labored on the report cover is probably not interested in your honest opinion. He probably seeks a compliment.

> Chances are, your spouse does not want to know it is almost midnight. The message is probably "I'm tired and would like to go home."

> The person planning a trip may actually be bragging that she's a world traveler. This may not be the time to bring up how much you enjoyed both countries two years ago.

We must look for hints in the questioner's tone of voice and body language in order to figure out the motive for the question. If in doubt, answering a question with a question often helps. "Are these keyboards dirty?" could be answered with "Do you want someone to clean them?"

Just as you must be careful how you answer questions, be careful how you phrase them. In fact, you may want to avoid questions in cases where direct communication is your aim. "I think our keyboards would look better if they were cleaned. I hope you can clean them by the end of the week" is not a veiled message. Instead of asking, "How did you get that done so quickly?" say, "I'm very pleased that you finished the report ahead of schedule." Asking a subordinate, "Are you busy this afternoon?" puts the unfortunate person at a disadvantage. What are you getting at? Do you want to pile on more work or take a long lunch together? **State your intentions or feelings up front.** "I'd like to buy you lunch. Is today a good day?" is effective communication.

Nolan Ryan is pitching much better
now that he has his curve ball straightened out.
—JOE GARAGIOLA

< *Saying No* >

One-half the troubles of this life can be traced
to saying yes too quickly and not saying no soon enough.
—JOSH BILLINGS

Let's face it, it's easier to say yes than to say no. We find ourselves saying yes to requests from children, spouses, neighbors, bosses, coworkers, and subordinates when we often wish we could say no. Some tips on saying no:

> Wear a poker face. **Listen attentively to requests, but show no positive or negative reaction.**

> **Do not respond immediately.** When the other person has finished talking, take a moment to consider. Then repeat the request in your own words to make sure you understand it. For instance, "It sounds like you want to change your work hours. Do you see this as a temporary or a permanent change?"

> **Ask for time.** After you fully understand the request, say something like "I want to think about this. I'll get back to you tomorrow." Be sure to keep your promise.

> **Think it over.** If you must deny the request, try developing alternatives that will meet everyone's needs.

> **Be gracious but firm.** Start the conversation by repeating the request. "I've thought about your request to change your work

hours. I'm not prepared to change our arrangements right now—I think we need you here during your current hours. I hope you're not disappointed."

> **Do not make excuses.** Don't blame higher-ups or whine about company policy. The less said, the better.

> **Ask for alternatives.** If you are open to other ideas, solicit them. Employees who are involved in developing a solution will be more committed to making it work.

> **Leave an "out."** You may want to say the request is worth reconsidering next month or next year or if conditions change.

> **Do not debate.** If pressed, responses like "I feel comfortable with my decision" or "I think this is best right now" are appropriate. If going into great detail will serve no purpose, don't do it.

There cannot be a crisis next week.
My schedule is already full.
—HENRY KISSINGER

< *Diversity* >

We must learn to live together as brothers or perish as fools.
—MARTIN LUTHER KING, JR.

A person's first job introduces them to many kinds of people they may have not met before. New employees often meet coworkers of different ages, religions, and ethnic backgrounds. The variety can be interesting, amusing—or unsettling. Here are some tips on how to accept and work with diverse people:

> Understand human nature. All of us have a natural tendency to pass judgment. We constantly seem to evaluate people and approve or disapprove of their words, demeanor, actions, and even possessions. If carried too far, this practice makes us critical, fault-finding, inflexible, and unpleasant. **Concentrate on noticing other people's strengths and abilities** not on what you perceive as their faults.

> Understand fear and hostility. If we are unfamiliar with how a person speaks, dresses, acts, and looks, we may feel uneasy around them. Unfortunately, this fear is often manifested as contempt, ridicule, or even hostility. **Try to see multicultural and other differences as an exciting opportunity to learn and experience new things.** You will also be able to see your own behavior and things you take for granted in a new light.

> Understand labeling. Before we even talk to people, we may like or dislike them. We give them the once-over and, based on the flimsiest of evidence, assign them to a category. We may use the color

of their skin, the way they wear their baseball cap, or the kind of jewelry they wear to pigeonhole them. Once we've labeled someone as a "bratty," "cold," or "opportunistic," we may view them thereafter through a lens that distorts them. This kind of stereotyping prevents us from really knowing them.

> **Recognize how illogical we can be.** After we get to know people better, they rarely fit the category we originally put them in. Rather than change our racial, cultural, or other stereotypical thinking, we somehow convince ourselves the people we've met are exceptions to the rule. **Despite evidence to the contrary, we hold on to our faulty thinking.**

> Turn the tables. **Others are labeling you, too.** Do you want your height, education, hair color, religion, or age to prevent them from seeing your essence? Worse, do you want this to be a factor in whether you're promoted? Use your open-mindedness to foster open-mindedness in others.

I am the inferior of any man whose rights I trample.
—HORACE GREELEY

< *Rumors and Gossip* >

Three may keep a secret, if two of them are dead.
—BENJAMIN FRANKLIN

People love to talk about other people. So, expect company grapevines to carry gossip about coworkers, rumors about office politics, and all kinds of "news." It's exciting to hear all the juicy details, but it's unwise to participate in every conversation. **It's fun to share secrets, but it's risky, too.** Here's why:

> **If your job gives you access to confidential or sensitive information, keep it to yourself.** It is essential to be known as a loyal and trustworthy employee.

> Making unkind remarks about others, even if true, makes you fair game for retaliation. You have no control over how many times your words will be repeated. Nor can you stop them from being garbled, exaggerated, or misunderstood. Assume that your remarks will find their way back to the person you spoke of. **Choose your comments as if they will be posted on the company bulletin board.**

> Scuttlebutt is seldom positive or uplifting. Some people like to spread bad news, speculate on what will happen next, and rehash every mistake your company and coworkers have made. Such pointless conversation wastes time and saps everyone's morale.

> **Grapevines are seldom reliable.** Spreading rumors and false information is no way to enhance your professional image.

> Idle chatter can take sudden twists. Innocent conversation about the company party can turn into critical or belittling talk about coworkers. If it does, excuse yourself by suddenly remembering a meeting or important phone call. **Your image as a person with class is a valuable asset. Maintain it.**

> Never share private or privileged information about friends. It's a sure way to ruin a friendship. And those you tell are smart to wonder what you say about them behind their backs.

> If a friend becomes the target of sharp tongues, stand up for them. Remaining silent is little better than joining in.

There is so much good in the worst of us,
and so much bad in the best of us,
that it behooves all of us not to talk about the rest of us.
—ROBERT LOUIS STEVENSON

< *Complaining* >

Any fool can criticize, condemn, and complain—
and most fools do.
—DALE CARNEGIE

Complaining is a common pastime in most offices. From your first
day on the job until your last, you'll hear complaints. Workers complain about management. They carp about the food in the cafeteria.
They groan about the workload. They squawk about pay. They gripe
about other departments. They grumble about coworkers. No topic
or person is spared.

**Just because complaining and saying uncomplimentary things
about others are common, and even if your statements are true or jus-
tified, don't pick up the habit. Here's why:**

> **Invariably the person you bad-mouth will find out about it.** At best,
   you will create an awkward situation. But if the worm turns, it
   could cost you a raise, promotion, or even your job.

> When you complain about the data processing department, you're
   criticizing the members of that team. After they find out about it,
   don't expect them to go out of their way to help you in a pinch.

> You run the risk of becoming a chronic complainer. **Those who
   enjoy pointing out real or imagined faults and imperfections are no
   fun to be around.** They aren't welcome in many office groups.

> You may develop a caustic wit and enjoy entertaining the troops. Coworkers may laugh when you mimic the boss. They'll probably chuckle at your clever, incisive remarks about someone who just left the room. However, they have every right to expect you to talk about them behind their backs. That makes you fair game, too.

> Organizations are complex, and workers often have limited flexibility in their jobs. **Instead of complaining about other employees and departments, cut them some slack. They may do the same for you.**

> Expressing frustration is healthy. **If you must say something to somebody, find a trustworthy listener.** Get it off your chest, say thanks for listening, then get back to work. When others need to let off steam, you play the listener's role. It's their show this time, so don't bring up your problems.

The reverse side also has a reverse side.
—JAPANESE PROVERB

< *Sexual Harassment* >

*Although words exist for the most part for the transmission of
ideas, there are some which produce such violent disturbance in
our feelings that the role they play in the transmission of
ideas is lost in the background.*
—ALBERT EINSTEIN

Behavior that was acceptable in the workplace a generation ago today
can cost you your job or land you in court. Ignorance of rules and
laws is no defense. In fact, the naive and unaware are in peril of sexu-
al harassment from both directions. They can be as easily accused of
it as subjected to it. Some advice:

> **Don't tell off-color jokes.** It's definitely risky in mixed company
and may be unwelcome in most situations. Using words with dou-
ble meanings can be equally offensive and repulsive.

> **Don't touch.** What you consider a friendly gesture could be con-
strued as something else. Witnesses can only explain what they saw.
They can't testify to your intentions.

> **Be careful with compliments.** Your comment about someone's fig-
ure or physique may be intended as a sincere compliment, but
could be regarded as demeaning or humiliating.

> **Don't flirt.** You may see flirting as harmless entertainment or even
an art. Others may see it as a veiled attempt to test the waters.

> **Don't even imply a proposition.** Making the slightest suggestion, even in jest, that a promotion, raise, or other benefit could be earned through sexual activity is the stuff of emotionally and financially costly lawsuits.

Remember not only to say the right thing in the right place, but far more difficult still, to leave unsaid the wrong thing at the tempting moment.

—BENJAMIN FRANKLIN

< *Gifts* >

Always go to other people's funerals, otherwise they won't come to yours.
—YOGI BERRA

Coworkers usually celebrate one another's weddings, promotions, retirements, and other milestones with gifts. Money is often collected by "passing the hat." Collections also take place to buy a holiday gift for the boss or to send flowers to a coworker who is hospitalized. Here are a few things to keep in mind when giving or receiving gifts:

Group giving:

> **Chip in.** It may seem like the hat is being passed quite often. You may also be asked to contribute for what you see as frivolous events. You'll be asked to help buy a present for someone you may not like. Nevertheless, contribute something. It will keep you in good standing with your coworkers.

Personal giving:

> For the boss. Some etiquette books suggest gifts for the boss. Others do not. If you prefer to give a gift during the holiday season or for a special occasion, select an appropriate one. A book, box of candy, or item related to a hobby is a good idea. Money, articles of clothing, gag gifts, or extravagant presents are not recommended.

> For a coworker. **If you've developed a strong friendship with one of your coworkers, gift giving should be done outside the office.**

This prevents others in the office from feeling left out.

Receiving gifts:

> **Be gracious.** Say something positive about the gift even if it runs counter to your taste or if you have one just like it. Remember to say thanks.

> **Send a note.** A note of thanks is appropriate when the gift was especially thoughtful or generous. If the gift was from a large group of coworkers, a note ensures that everyone is thanked. Such notes are often posted on the departmental bulletin board for all to see. The note need not be long. It should be enthusiastic and specifically mention the gift you received.

Declining gifts:

> From customers. **Review your company's policy about accepting gifts from suppliers.** It is better to politely decline an expensive gift from a supplier than to have your impartiality put to the test or questioned.

> From admirers. **If Cupid causes an admirer to step forward with an expensive and unwanted gift, do not accept it.** Be tactful but decisive. "How thoughtful and generous of you, but I simply can't accept" is sufficient.

If you treat people right, they will treat you right—
90 percent of the time.
—FRANKLIN ROOSEVELT

< *Using the Telephone* >

For three days after death, hair and fingernails continue to grow but phone calls taper off.
—JOHNNY CARSON

Telephones are so common that it is easy to take them for granted. However, they are an important business-communications tool. Some tips on using this tool:

Answering your telephone:

> **Answer as soon as possible.** Allowing the phone to ring four or more times gives the impression of poor staffing.

> **Answer with a warm, confident, enthusiastic voice.** "Al Eilers" or "Sales department, Mr. Eilers speaking" works well.

Placing a telephone call:

> **Beware of background noise.** Close your door or turn down the radio before placing the call.

> **Do not eat or chew gum while on the phone.** Cover the mouthpiece if a sneeze or cough is unavoidable—then apologize for the interruption.

> **Immediately identify yourself.** Secretaries and receptionists appreciate this approach: "Good morning, this is Frank Doerger from Rainbow WetWare, calling Mr. Eilers."

> Speak distinctly and slowly when giving your phone number or spelling your name.

> **If disconnected, call back.** The convention is for callers to call back regardless of who or what caused the disconnection.

> **Keep it short and sweet.** Assume that the other person is busy. You may want to ask if this is a convenient time for the call. If so, get to the point and end the conversation. If you've caught the person at a bad time, ask when it would be a good time to call back.

> **Give the person your undivided attention.** Speaking to someone else in the room or typing on your computer is not only distracting, it's impolite.

> Don't act curious. If the person you are trying to reach is not in, do not ask where they are. If you want to call back, you may want to ask, "Do you think this afternoon would be a good time for me to call back?"

> **Leave a specific message if the person you are trying to reach is not available.** For instance, say "Let Mr. Bacon know I'm calling to learn the status of the Scott report." Not only does this save Mr. Bacon time when he returns your call, but the person taking the message may be able to help.

> **Be polite if interrupted during a conversation.** Say "Excuse me for a minute." Cover the phone's mouthpiece and take care of the problem. Say "Sorry," and then continue the conversation.

> **Let the person on the other end know if you are using a speaker-phone.** This cautions them that the conversation may not be private.

Answering someone else's telephone:

> **Identify yourself.** "Mr. Bacon's extension, Frank Doerger speaking" or "Finance department, Frank Doerger speaking" says it all.

> **Ask for a message:** "Mr. Jones is not in the office. Can I take a message?" Then write down the day, date, and time of the call. Be sure to get the caller's name, area code, telephone number, and extension. It's a good idea to read these back to the caller to make sure the information is correct.

> **Write legibly.** If necessary, neatly rewrite the message before passing it along.

Returning telephone calls:

> **Do so within 24 hours.** It is common business courtesy to return all calls within this time span. If you are on vacation or out of the office for a few days, those who answer your phone should relate this information to callers.

> **State the reason for your call:** "This is Frank Doerger returning Mr. Eilers' call" or "Al, this is Frank Doerger returning your call."

Leaving voice mail:

> **Be pleasant, brief, but thorough:** "Hello, Mr. Jones, Scott Dunn calling from Rainbow WetWare about your recent order. It's Tuesday at 10:30 A.M. I'll try to reach you later. If you want to reach me, I'm at 999-574-2697 until 5:30 P.M. today." Speak slowly, especially when giving your phone number.

Transferring a call:

> If a caller has reached the wrong extension, offer to transfer them to the correct number. **Tell the caller the correct extension in case they are disconnected during the transfer.** That way the call can be placed directly.

> *Well, if I called the wrong number,*
> *why did you answer the phone?*
> —JAMES THURBER

< *Doors and Elevators* >

Always do right. This will gratify some people and astonish the rest.
—MARK TWAIN

Your manners are on display in public places. Make the right impression as you move from place to place in the office, shop floor, parking lot, or lobby. Here's how:

> Walk on the right-hand side of hallways and stairwells. **Round corners slowly so you don't run into someone coming the other way.**

> **If you are leading the way with a group and approach a door that pushes open, push it open and walk through.** You may want to hold the door for those behind you.

> If the door pulls open, hold it open for those behind you.

> If you are first to get to a revolving door, go through and wait for the rest of the group on the other side.

> If you are driving, unlock the passengers' doors before getting in.

> If an elevator is crowded, the person closest to the door exits first.

> Before getting on an elevator, allow those getting off to do so before you step in.

> If you are on an elevator and closest to the control panel, ask which floors need to be punched. Hold the door open or press the "Open" button until everyone is safely in or out. **Hold the elevator door or hold the "Open" button for people coming down the hall.**

We are all born charming, fresh, and spontaneous and must be civilized before we are fit to participate in society.
—MISS MANNERS (JUDITH MARTIN)

TEAMWORK

< *Being a Valuable Employee* >

*The ability to deal with people is as purchasable a commodity
as sugar or coffee. And I pay more for that ability
than for any other under the sun.*
—JOHN D. ROCKEFELLER

Good employees are a company's most valuable asset. Here's how to be as well as project the image of an employee your company wants on its team:

> **Be punctual.** If your starting time is 8:00 A.M., be at your workstation and ready to work at 8:00 A.M. (Pulling into the parking lot at 8:00 or settling in from 8:00 to 8:15 isn't the same thing.) Arriving early gives the impression that you're eager to start your work.

> Don't report for duty and then routinely eat breakfast, apply make-up, or telephone the baby-sitter. Do those things before starting time.

> **If you are sick or otherwise unable to go to work, call in.** Do the same thing if it looks like you will be considerably late.

> **Be loyal to your boss.** Don't tell others about his mistakes, foibles, or personal problems. Remember, there's a good chance your

remarks will find their way back to him. Disloyal or untrustworthy employees may find it difficult to be promoted. If you say anything about your boss, say something positive.

> **Keep your desk and work area neat.** Keeping things in their proper place not only presents a professional image, but it also makes it easier for your boss and others to find things in your absence.

> **Be cordial to visitors.** Help promote an atmosphere that makes clients and customers feel welcome.

> **Be patient and understanding toward other employees.** You'll spend much time with them, and it will pay in the long run to be known as a team player.

> **Keep confidential matters confidential.** If you can't be trusted with small matters, you will not be trusted with large ones.

> **Protect your boss from surprises.** If you make a big mistake or if a major project under your control falls behind schedule, tell your boss. It will be better for you if you step forward with the news. You don't want your boss to be caught off guard by having bad news reach her secondhand.

> **Solve little problems yourself.** Most bosses don't want to hear about every obstacle and difficulty. They want to spend their time doing their job, and they expect you to do yours.

> **Take responsibility when things go wrong.** Blaming others and making excuses is not a sign of strength or self-confidence. If it happened on your watch, say so, and make sure it doesn't happen again.

> **Make your boss look good.** If your boss trusts you to prepare a report, make sure it reflects well on both of you. If it doesn't, don't be surprised if someone else is asked to prepare a report the next time.

> Work. Remember, you are paid to produce. **Limit personal phone calls and time away from your work area.**

> **Do what you say you will.** If you say the report will be finished on Friday, do everything you can to keep your promise. Failure to follow through—even on little things—makes bosses wonder if you'll be reliable on big assignments.

> **Try to beat deadlines.** If it's due on Friday, finish it on Thursday. Meeting or beating deadlines indicates commitment and good planning.

> **Dress appropriately, which usually means following the boss' lead.** Dressing "a level up" gives the impression that you want to move up. But do it with finesse. Dressing beyond your means or current position can project the wrong image.

Hard work never killed anybody, but why take the chance?
—CHARLIE McCARTHY (EDGAR BERGEN)

< *Being a Good Coworker* >

One of the best ways to persuade others is with your ears—
by listening to them.
—Dean Rusk

Your success, the success of your area or department, and your fellow employees' success will depend on the ability of all of you to work together effectively. Equally important, many of your waking hours will be spent with your fellow workers. Here are some ways to make those hours productive and pleasant:

> **Congratulate others on their successes and promotions.** If you can't be sincere and genuine, don't fake it.

> Compliment coworkers on a job well done.

> Say good morning and good night to coworkers, and return their greetings.

> **Learn coworkers' first and last names, as well as how to spell them.** You will quickly make friends on your second encounter if you can call people by their names.

> **Respect the privacy of others.** Do not read their mail or anything at their workstation. Do not give the impression that you are trying to overhear their conversations. If you do overhear someone's conversation, never repeat it.

> Do not ask coworkers to warn you when the boss is coming or to otherwise "cover" for you.

> **Do not pry into coworkers' personal lives.** If someone shares something personal with you, it is because they believe you are trustworthy. It is important to live up to this expectation.

> Do not brag about your education, upbringing, accomplishments, possessions, or children.

> Do not tell off-color, sexist, or racist jokes or stories. Racy stories or jokes with sexual innuendoes can be construed as sexual harassment.

> **Stay out of feuds and arguments.** Taking sides will come back to haunt you.

> Apologize as soon as possible after offending someone.

> Resist the temptation to complain about other departments.

> Settle differences in private.

> If you are not busy, don't roam about chitchatting. Find something to do.

> **If you are long-winded, work hard at becoming more brief.** Deal with "talkers" with a polite "I'm sorry, but I must get back to this task."

> **Don't borrow large amounts of money from or lend large amounts of money to coworkers.** However, by all means, help out those who forgot money for lunch or parking.

> **Don't gossip.** It's best to assume that anything you say could be repeated.

> **Be aware of annoying and distracting habits.** Don't crack your knuckles, display uncovered yawns, belch, chew on pens, clip nails, or sit on someone's desk.

> Make more coffee if you take the last cup. **Clean up if you make a mess in the vending area.**

> **If you're permitted to listen to music, it should be appropriate for the setting, and played softly.** Ask if others find it distracting. If so, turn it off.

One hand cannot applaud alone.
—ARABIAN PROVERB

< *Being Assigned a Task* >

The fool wonders, the wise man asks.
—BENJAMIN DISRAELI

Sometimes bosses assign tasks in writing, but generally, they simply tell staff to do something. This is often done on the spur of the moment or in a casual way. Doing the job correctly depends a great deal on your understanding of the mission. Bosses are usually hard-pressed for time and have many things on their minds. So, they don't always give clear assignments. Here's how to minimize misunderstandings and confusion:

> **If your boss calls you to her office, bring a pencil and paper.** Take notes.

> If your boss approaches your work area, stop what you are doing and grab a pencil and paper. **Listen carefully and take notes.**

> Your notes should include who, what, when, where, and why.

> **Make sure you know when the task is to be completed.** If your boss uses words like "soon" or "when you can get to it," seek clarification. Soon may mean next week to you and tomorrow to him. Ask "Will the end of the day tomorrow be soon enough?"

> **If your boss gives you a tight deadline, it's OK to remind her of other tasks you are working on so this new task can be assigned a priority.** It's appropriate to ask "Should I put this ahead of the

marketing project?" This is also a handy way to remind your boss of your other projects.

> **If the task requires others to be involved, ask if the other employees know about this task and its priority.** A good boss will make sure you have the resources available to complete the job. Be careful not to assume authority over others because your boss assigned an important project to you. Emphasize cooperation and team effort.

> **Review your notes, and repeat to your boss what you think you've just been asked to do.** This is the time to make sure there are no misunderstandings.

> **End the conversation on a confident note.** Say "I'll get started right away" or "Consider it done."

> **If the task is a large or complicated one, let your boss know how things are going.** If it's on schedule, say so. If things aren't going well or if you're unsure of how to proceed, talk to your boss. Don't wait until the last minute to admit you're in over your head.

> **Meet or beat the deadline**—even if it means finishing the job on your own time.

> **When you turn the project in, ask if there is anything else you can do to help.** Bosses like to know you are ready, willing, and able to chip in.

It is not enough to be busy; so are the ants.
The question is: What are we busy about?
—HENRY DAVID THOREAU

< *Accepting Praise* >

People ask for criticism, but they only want praise.
—SOMERSET MAUGHAM

The proper reaction to praise can leave everyone feeling good. However, if you're not sure how to react to praise, kind words from your boss could backfire into an awkward moment. You may even give the impression that you're rejecting the compliment. Some tips on how to gracefully accept praise:

> Don't remain mute or downplay your accomplishment with a meek "It was nothing."

> **A confident "thank-you" acknowledges that you're proud of your efforts.** You may want to add something like "That's nice of you to say" or "That's good to hear" or "I'm glad I was able to help."

> If others helped you or deserve some credit, a comment like "Fred and Juanita contributed a lot" shows you're a team player.

> **Tell those who helped you earn the praise that your boss was pleased.** Let them know you appreciate their help.

Having the critics praise you
is like having the hangman say you've got a pretty neck.
—ELI WALLACH

< *Getting Along With the Boss* >

By working faithfully eight hours a day,
you may eventually get to be a boss and work twelve hours a day.
—Robert Frost

The happiness of your work life will depend greatly on your relationships with bosses. Of course, they have the advantage in the boss–worker relationship. However, you can influence it to your benefit. Here's how:

> **Don't be too chummy.** A boss is not your buddy, friend, or confessor. He has power and authority over you. Do not discuss personal problems or ask for advice on personal matters. Aim for a professional relationship.

> Study your boss. Some thrive on stress, some don't. Some take interruptions in stride, other don't. Some are morning people, others hit their stride later in the day. Some are sticklers for details. Others like to see the big picture. Some are neat freaks. Some place much value on promptness. **Understand your boss and get in sync with her rhythm.**

> **Accept the climate your boss sets.** It may be formal, informal, competitive, cooperative. If it's different from your natural bent, try to adapt. In some cases, your example could rub off on your boss, but don't count on it.

> Keep in mind that your boss also has a boss. Your boss has a wider range of responsibilities, problems, and difficulties than you do. **Try to see things from his point of view.**

> **Don't expect a perfect boss.** Give her the same degree of understanding you expect.

> **Respect the chain of command.** Going around or over your boss is a dangerous move. Keep him informed. If your boss' boss asks you to do something, let your boss know.

> **Be loyal to your boss.** A loyal team player is a valuable asset to any manager. If you have a difficult boss, other bosses just may notice your good attitude under trying conditions and help you transfer to their department.

> *Be awful nice to 'em going up,*
> *because you're gonna meet 'em comin' down.*
> —JIMMY DURANTE

< *Dealing With a Difficult Boss* >

I'm not the type to get ulcers. I give them.
—EDWARD J. KOCH

Bosses are people, too, and they each have a unique combination of strengths and weaknesses. Their strengths may include good leadership, communication, motivational, and technical skills. Traits like decisiveness, a sense of humor, and patience are strengths, too. Weaknesses might include poor planning skills, a short temper, and a tendency to play favorites among subordinates. Here are some ways to deal with a difficult boss:

> **Be patient.** Most bosses are promoted to management because they performed well in a nonmanagement position. They may not have received training in managing and motivating others. If your boss is new at managing people, allow him some time to acquire on-the-job training. **Remember, being a boss is a tough job.**

> **Be assertive.** Some bosses use fear as a management technique. They may raise their voice, move about in a huff, and use foul, belittling, or abusive language. Many bullies back down when confronted by a formidable opponent. Counter with eye contact, body language, and voice inflection that suggest they should find someone else to pick on. Another strategy is to reason with your boss. After the storm has abated, explain that "It doesn't help when others get very upset with me because I take it personally and find it hard to concentrate on my work."

> **Make suggestions.** Some bosses find it hard to set priorities or make decisions. Help your boss by indirectly taking charge yourself. Say, "A computer network makes sense. What do you think? Want me to look into the advantages?" Use an approach that will get the job done without offending your boss or appearing to usurp her power.

> **Mention the big picture.** The boss who is a perfectionist can waste everyone's time and destroy morale. Routine letters and memos may go through three revisions before mailing. Every task must be checked and rechecked. Everything is nitpicked; nothing is done quite right, and everyone is over-supervised. Improve your productivity and morale by reminding your boss of the important things that must be accomplished. If you think you're being asked to spend time on the wrong thing, say "I also need to finish the sales report. Which do you think I should do first?" Hopefully, such comments will put things back in perspective.

> **Motivate yourself.** Some bosses rarely compliment subordinates and limit their feedback to criticism. Counter this lopsided approach by reminding yourself of your noteworthy accomplishments and positive traits.

> **Don't slack off.** It's tempting to let the quantity and quality of your work dip when you work for a difficult boss. It's an understandable reaction but poor strategy. Your reputation and performance reviews are likely to suffer. It may even cost you your job.

> **Become indispensable.** Closely study your boss to find out how you can be of greatest value to him. Does he want help planning,

organizing, writing? Does he have fears and insecurities? Does he need a confidant, cheerleader, sounding board? Does he enjoy talking about his travels? Would he prefer that someone else take care of details? Become a valuable career partner, and your working relationship is likely to be a rewarding one—even with a "terrible" boss.

> Be honest. **You are fully one-half of the relationship.** Put yourself in the boss' shoes and imagine how she would describe you to her replacement. Are you dependable? Hardworking? Loyal? Knowledgeable? A team player? **Work on improving any weaknesses.**

It does not do to leave a live dragon out of your calculations,
if you live near him.
—J.R. TOLKIEN

LEADERSHIP

< *Conducting a Meeting* >

*A committee is a cul-de-sac down which ideas are lured
and then quietly strangled.*
—SIR BARNETT COCKS

Millions of meetings will be held throughout the business world next week. Some will be productive, but many will not. Here are a few tips to increase your chances of holding painless and productive meetings:

> **Use a memo or E-mail to announce the date, time, location, and agenda of the meeting.** Do this well in advance of the meeting. Pick an appropriate day and time. You may want to avoid late afternoon because energy levels may be low. You may also want to avoid days immediately before or after a three-day weekend. State the purpose of the meeting and what you hope to accomplish. Include the agenda and how much time you expect to spend on each topic.

> **Consider calling or E-mailing participants a few days before the meeting to remind them** of the date, time, and place. If you expect to schedule a follow-up meeting, ask participants to bring their calendars so a date and time can be set.

> Choose a location that is quiet and uncluttered.

> **Arrive at the meeting's location early enough to make sure the door is open, the temperature is comfortable, there are enough chairs, and the audiovisual equipment works.** Ensure there are no impediments.

> Bring extra copies of the agenda for those who arrive without theirs.

> Make introductions as people arrive, and do what you can to break the ice.

> **Start on time.** Waiting for latecomers encourages tardiness. Acknowledge them by telling them you'll fill them in later on what they missed.

> Open the meeting by stating what you hope to achieve and how long you've estimated each agenda item will take.

> **Stick to the agenda.** It may be necessary to restate the meeting's purpose in order to keep the discussion from drifting off course.

> **Use open-ended questions to encourage comments from all present.** "How do you see it, Gloria?" and "What would you like to add, Sam?" are examples. Another way to elicit feedback from everyone is to go around the table, asking each person for ideas.

> **Discourage anyone from dominating the discussion.** Here is one way to give the floor to someone else: "Paul, it sounds like you prefer buying instead of leasing. How do you see it, Claire?"

> Break after long sessions to give everyone a chance to stretch their legs, refresh themselves, and make phone calls.

> **Close the meeting by summarizing what has been accomplished.** Encourage each participant to state what they will do and when. This helps generate commitment.

> **Thank those who attended.** Give special recognition to those who made presentations. Don't forget to give credit to those who may have assisted in arranging the meeting.

> If a follow-up meeting is to be scheduled, decide on its agenda.

> **Check with those who are working on tasks to be completed before the next meeting.** If they are having difficulties, offer assistance or alternatives to ensure deadlines will be met.

> Distribute minutes as soon as practical.

> Consider how to improve the meeting process.

> *To negotiate: to seek a meeting of minds*
> *without a knocking together of heads.*
> —ERIC SEVAREID

< *Making Decisions* >

It is a capital mistake to theorize before one has data.
—SHERLOCK HOLMES (SIR ARTHUR CONAN DOYLE)

The world of work may seem like an unending series of problems, challenges, and opportunities. You'll be asked to handle most situations by drawing upon your education, experience, and judgment. Employers expect important decisions with far-reaching consequences to be made by using a more formal decision- or problem-solving process. Here's one:

> **Define the problem.** This step is crucial because it determines your approach. It's common to mistake symptoms for problems. Investigate the situation until you fully understand the root causes. **Because it's easy to jump to erroneous conclusions, challenge your assumptions.** Because a computer printer jams repeatedly doesn't necessarily mean the printer is broken. Perhaps you're using the wrong kind of paper. Describe problems in writing, which helps reveal faulty or incomplete thinking.

> **List potential solutions.** Difficult or stubborn problems may require creative approaches. **Ask others for ideas.** Find out how similar situations were handled in the past. **Try brainstorming.**

> **Evaluate solutions.** Consider the pros and cons of several possible answers. If no clear winner emerges, develop a point system to grade potential solutions. For instance, each solution could earn

from one to ten points for cost, effort, risk, and time to implement. The winner is the option with the highest number of points.

> **Decide on a course of action.** If necessary, inform your boss and get her approval before you move ahead. **Ask yourself, "Who else needs to know?"** Tell others who may be affected by your plan, and solicit their support by taking the time to explain the situation. Anticipate how your actions will affect other departments and especially customers.

> Implement your ideas. **Time permitting, test your solution on a small scale.** Instead of buying ten printers, test one for a few weeks to see if it meets your expectations. If not, try another model.

> **Monitor results.** Periodically check to make sure the solution is working. Listen for meaningful feedback and be willing to modify your approach if the evidence warrants it. Be prepared for complaints because decisions seldom satisfy all involved. **Be flexible, but don't expect to please everyone—it can't be done.**

After all is said and done, more is said than done.
—UNKNOWN

< *Selling Ideas* >

I steer my bark with hope in the head, leaving fear astern.
—THOMAS JEFFERSON

How an idea is presented to management and coworkers often determines whether it will be accepted. Here are some tips on selling your ideas:

> **Do your homework.** Make sure your idea isn't exactly the same one that failed miserably six months ago. Find out what other suggestions were made and rejected. Discern which attempts failed and why. Determine if the situation has changed since the last "solution."

> **Get "buy in." Before you formally present your idea, consult with others who may be affected by your proposed changes.** They will be more supportive if you've conferred with them and sought their opinion. This will also give you a feel for those who may later oppose your plan.

> Describe the problem. **Convince others that there really is a problem before you try to sell them a solution.** They'll see the merits of your idea if they understand the situation as well as you do.

> **Describe who will benefit.** Cynics will wonder just how you'll benefit from your own idea. Some may even think you have something up your sleeve. Explain who would benefit if the situation were

magically improved. Focus on increased sales, customer satisfaction, and reduced expenses.

> Describe your idea. **Be clear and concise.** Use language everyone understands, and present the solution from the listeners' point of view. Don't say "We need a Pentium 100 MHz computer with an internal modem." Say "A computer will allow us to send data over the phone lines and eliminate overnight delivery fees."

> **Use key words.** If the powers that be stress customer satisfaction, emphasize the part of your plan that will appeal to customers. If the organization seeks to reduce costs, mention how your idea fits into the organization's overall cost-containment effort.

> **List the drawbacks.** Most solutions have disadvantages. **Don't ignore or try to hide them.** Mention them! Say something like "Of course, the computer will cost almost $1,500, and we will need to train someone to use it. But reduced delivery fees will pay for the computer in one year. We'll also be able to use it for other tasks."

> Agree with the critics. Expect others to look for flaws in your idea. **Don't be defensive.** Instead, acknowledge their points by using phrases like "Good point. I looked into that and discovered…" or "That concerned me, too. I suspect that…"

> **Avoid the word "but." Instead of saying "I see your point, but…" say "I see your point, and I also think…"** The word "but" gives the impression of downplaying the initial comment. The word "and" gives the impression you are elaborating on it.

> Ask for permission to start. Don't settle for simply making a good presentation. **If your boss seems receptive, try for some kind of commitment.** Ask "Should I take the first step?" or "Will you sign the purchase order?" or "Should I get started tomorrow?"

Four things come not back—the spoken word, the sped arrow, the past life, and the neglected opportunity.
—ARABIAN PROVERB

< *Offering Constructive Criticism* >

See everything, overlook a great deal, correct a little.
—POPE JOHN XXIII

We often hope problems will go away if left alone. But if ignored, problems tend to grow worse. Not confronting a problem—such as an employee who is chronically late—only reinforces the poor work habit. **We lose the respect of others in the office when we ignore problems. Some tips:**

> **Make sure of your facts.** Also make sure criticism is needed and appropriate. It does no good correcting, reminding, and confronting everyone about every little thing. However, if the behavior affects productivity, profits, morale, your image, or if it simply drives you to distraction, do something.

> **Do not complain about one employee to another.** It is unprofessional, and will likely become common knowledge and affect morale.

> **Remember that others cannot read your mind and may have no idea you consider their behavior unacceptable.** It's doubtful they are intent on irritating you.

> **Don't criticize things beyond a person's control.** If someone is not skilled enough to master the new software, make other provisions or don't mention it.

> **Your aim is to help the person improve.** It is not to judge or belittle.

> **Consider the personality of the employee to be talked to.** Will a gentle reminder or a stern reprimand be most effective?

> **It may be helpful to practice what you plan to say.** You may also want to prepare responses to questions or comments.

> Select a time and place that is convenient and private.

> Express yourself in a calm, collected manner. State the facts and their repercussions: "When people are chronically late it makes it difficult for me to manage the office." **Speak adult to adult, using positive terms.** Instead of "Stop being late," say "Begin arriving on time."

> **Stick to one incident,** and don't use the terms "never" or "always" in describing behavior.

> **Try to use phrases that are nonjudgmental.** Instead of "You are too talkative," say "I've noticed you are often on the phone to friends and for long periods of time."

> **End the session by summarizing** what has been said. Agree on how things will be done in the future.

> **Reinforce future positive behavior.** Let employees know you have recognized their efforts and progress.

People who fight fire with fire usually end up with ashes.
—ABIGAIL VAN BUREN

< *Asserting Yourself* >

Never argue; repeat your assertion.
—ROBERT OWEN

In many situations involving others, we tend to be submissive, aggressive, or assertive. Most of us are probably submissive. We're slow to confront others when they ignore our rights and feelings or otherwise take advantage of us. On the other hand, aggressive people try to have their way even if it's at the expense of others. **Assertive people protect themselves from being taken advantage of, while simultaneously respecting themselves and others. Here's a crash course in assertiveness training:**

> **Be realistic.** Many of us silently endure having our rights, opinions, and feelings tread on. We secretly hope the situation will somehow improve on its own. Chances are, it won't.

> **Be generous.** Don't assume people know they are infringing on your "personal space." A coworker may be unaware that his constant whistling distracts and prevents you from concentrating on your work.

> **Be optimistic.** It's easy to think that standing up for yourself will cause hard feelings and worsen the situation. The right approach can actually improve relationships.

> **Be prepared.** After you've decided to assert yourself, write out what you plan to say. This will clarify your thinking. It may also diffuse

strong feelings. A "dry run" with a friend or family member may ready you for a variety of reactions.

> **Make an appointment.** This strategy makes it clear that you have something important to discuss. Without an appointment, a co-worker can easily cut you short by saying they don't have the time to talk to you.

> **Get to the point.** Immediately state your purpose. Starting with friendly chitchat doesn't set a serious enough stage. Say something like "I'd like to talk to you about how I feel when coworkers are late for an appointment."

> State your case. **Calmly and confidently state three things: the questionable behavior, how it makes you feel, and, finally, the effect the behavior has.** For instance, "When people are habitually twenty minutes late for appointments, I feel frustrated because it throws me off my schedule and I can't get my work done." Don't blame or find fault. Concentrate on the situation and your feelings—not on the person causing them.

> **Pause to listen.** This is also part of your strategy. Rambling on weakens your case. In addition, letting the other person talk gives them a chance to diffuse their feelings.

> **Restate what you've heard.** None of us like to find out we're causing problems for others, so defensiveness is natural. Listen to the other side of the story and restate it. Repeating a position minimizes misunderstandings. Sometimes it helps others see the weakness in their thinking.

> **Don't become sidetracked.** Be prepared for a wide range of responses that might easily deflect you from your purpose. You might face rebuttals, questions, excuses, anger, tears, silence, hostility, and accusations. Don't allow yourself to be pulled into the tar pit. Restate what you hear the other person saying. Get back on track by reasserting your original statement. The other person's defensiveness will decrease if you can avoid becoming defensive yourself. If your coworker grows too upset, suggest discussing the issue again at a specific time.

> **Make an agreement.** "So, you'll set the alarm on your watch to alert you to make our appointments. Agreed?"

> **Follow up.** It's difficult for people to alter their behavior. One discussion often does not get the job done. If not, be assertive, and start the process over again.

*Snow and adolescence are the only problems that disappear
if you ignore them long enough.*
—EARL WILSON

< *Brainstorming* >

Each thought that is welcomed and recorded is like a nest egg,
by the side of which more will be laid.
—HENRY DAVID THOREAU

Before you or your work team makes a major decision, you'll want to feel comfortable that you have considered a wide range of possibilities. **Brainstorming, perhaps the easiest and most enjoyable way to come up with ideas, is a planned, free-form session that lets people be creative.** It's often a fun, exciting way to generate ideas. Here's how to do it:

> Get ready. **Consider holding the session outside the department, which promotes a fresh outlook.** Provide comfortable chairs. Have a flip chart, chalkboard, or large paper available for recording ideas. Write the purpose of the brainstorming session on the flip chart or in a way that is visible to all. You may want to state your ideas as questions: "How can we speed up the distribution of important reports?" "How can we get data to those who need it in a more timely manner?"

> **Create a relaxed atmosphere, but make it clear from the beginning that everyone is expected to participate.** Explain brainstorming rules. Consider posting them for everyone to see.

Brainstorming rules:

> Encourage as many ideas as possible—even silly ones.

> Do not discuss the merits of ideas—the goal is to maintain a creative, freewheeling atmosphere.

> Encourage participants to "hitchhike" or "piggyback" on each others' ideas.

> Write all ideas on the flip chart in letters large enough so everyone can see them. Having every idea visible helps to inspire more ideas.

> Start with a minute or two of silence to give everyone a chance to think about the purpose of the session.

> **Ask participants to call out their ideas.** Depending on the group and the purpose, consider other approaches. You may want to take turns offering ideas. You may ask everyone to write down their ideas, then take turns reading them.

> Encourage silly, expensive, outrageous ideas. Look for ways to combine suggestions.

> Humor seems to help generate ideas. **Encourage jokes and funny remarks to keep the energy high and the laughs coming.**

> **Record the ideas on the flip chart.** The recorder should refrain from interpreting the ideas but should instead write the exact words of the person making the suggestion.

> When everyone is out of ideas, ask for one more from each person.

> After you've completed your list, reduce it to one or a few worth trying. Multivoting is one way to do that. Voting is important because it reduces the possibility that an idea is chosen because a high-ranking or vocal person thought of it. **Voting improves "buy in" from the group.** Here's how it works:

- Combine similar items but only if everyone agrees they are the same.
- Number all items so participants can refer to them by number. This saves time and reduces confusion.
- Vote. Each member votes for every idea they consider worthy of continued attention.
- Discuss your purpose and the top vote-getters.
- Vote and discuss the ideas again until only a few remain.
- **Choose the idea the group thinks has the best chance for success.**

> If possible, first test the solution on a small scale. If the test proves promising, use what you learned during the test to go full scale. If the test is disappointing, try the solution that received the next highest number of votes.

Welcome all ideas and entertain them royally,
for one of them may be king.
—MARK VAN DOREN

< *Being a Good Boss* >

Morale is the greatest single factor in successful wars.
—DWIGHT D. EISENHOWER

A person is placed in a position of authority in order to get the job done. High morale in a team setting is the best way to achieve good results. A few reminders for bosses:

> Let employees know how you prefer to be addressed. Find out how they prefer to be addressed.

> Praise in public. Criticize in private.

> **Share the credit.** Most successes result from team effort. If your own boss congratulates you, let him or her know you couldn't have done it without the other members of your team.

> **Give employees the tools needed to do the job.** Management controls all resources. You wouldn't attempt to repair a car without the correct tools and equipment. Don't expect your employees to accomplish a comparable task without the proper resources.

> **Address problems quickly.** Ignoring problems or taking weeks or months to address them gives the impression you have little interest in your team's well-being.

> **Solicit ideas.** Work is complex, and those who are closest to it are in the best position to offer ideas. Similarly, when you ask someone

to do something, give them the background and reasons to help them make good decisions.

> Make sure someone can fill in for you when you're absent. Do not give your boss or your customers the impression that your area drifts aimlessly when you are away. **Give your team the training, means, and authority to deal with problems in your absence.**

> **Don't play favorites.** It undermines morale and team cooperation.

> **Keep your staff informed** of activity in the department, division, and company. Don't let rumors be their only source of information.

> Let workers know how they are doing. You are more than a boss. You are also a coach and teacher. **Give your staff feedback and support to help them improve not only for your team but for their personal well-beings.**

The secret of managing is to keep the guys who hate you away from the guys who are undecided.
—CASEY STENGEL

< *Assigning a Task* >

*Never tell people how to do things. Tell them what to do
and they will surprise you with their ingenuity.*
—GENERAL GEORGE S. PATTON

How well a task is explained and understood greatly influences how
well it will be done. Some tips:

> **Plan.** Before you assign a task, think about it. What needs to be
done? Why? By when? What are the potential pitfalls?

> **Write it down.** Anything but the simplest task should include writ-
ten notes. Although the notes could be for your benefit, you'll
probably want to give a copy of them to the person you're assign-
ing the task. **The task's who, what, when, where, and why should
be clear to all involved.**

> Assign the task. **Take time to fully explain the project.** A few extra
minutes spent at the outset can easily save hours caused by misunderstandings and confusion. Time spent planning the effort also
indicates that the task is important.

> **State the purpose.** Employees are better able to make suggestions
and decisions if they know the "big picture" and how each task fits
into it.

> **Be specific.** Don't use vague terms like "soon" or "when you find
the time." Say "by noon tomorrow" or "by the end of the day."

> **Agree on how long it will take.** Estimate the effort involved. "Do you think you can get the job done in about four hours?" indicates how long you think it may take. Of course, you may be wrong or have underestimated just how much you're asking. Discuss it with your staff.

> **Assign a priority.** Your task will likely be one of several your staff will be juggling. Assign a priority to this latest task. "Put this ahead of the budget project" leaves no doubt as to which is more important.

> **Supply the necessary resources.** If the task requires a computer, make sure one is available. If it requires the cooperation of other workers, introduce them to one another. Do what you can to "grease the wheels."

> **Share your expertise.** If you know a tip or shortcut that will make the task easier, share it. However, let your staff choose how to tackle the task. This is important for a couple of reasons: first, it shows your confidence in them, and second, they may already know or may discover a better way to get the job done.

> **Ask if there are questions.** But go beyond the standard "Do you understand?" Use open-ended questions like "Which part do you think will be most time-consuming?" Listen for hints that indicate the task is fully understood.

> **Offer assistance.** Tell your staff to see you if they have trouble or feel uncertain about what to do. If you will be on vacation or otherwise unavailable, make sure they know who may be able to answer questions.

> **Stay in touch.** Check on progress to make sure everything is going as you expect. Don't wait until the task was done incorrectly to find out you were misunderstood. Consider scheduling periodic progress meetings.

> **Critique. Feedback is important.** Tell your staff what you thought of their work. Mention high points, but do not ignore areas that need improvement. It is unfair to give the impression that all went well when it didn't. Suggest how it could be done better next time, and improvements will likely happen.

Great discoveries and improvements invariably involve
the cooperation of many minds.
—ALEXANDER GRAHAM BELL

< *Continuous Quality Improvement* >

There's a way to do it better—find it.
—THOMAS EDISON

Total Quality Improvement, Total Quality Management, and Continuous Quality Improvement are names commonly applied to an increasingly popular kind of management philosophy. This style of managing is frequently given credit for the growth of the Japanese economy.

Many businesses in the United States have embraced the quality movement. **Because this approach and its terminology are common, it helps to know the basics:**

> **Organizations must be customer driven.** Meeting and exceeding customer needs and expectations is all-important.

> Everything the company does (called processes or systems) must start and end with the customer in mind.

> Improvements reduce costs, which results in lower prices. Lower prices mean increased sales.

> Working closely with suppliers and customers improves the chances of satisfying customers.

> By nature, people want to do their job well and look for better ways to get things done.

> **The person performing a job is probably more knowledgeable about it than anyone else.** It helps to seek their opinion on matters affecting their job.

> **Workers can do a better job when they understand why they do what they do.** Seeing the big picture helps them make independent decisions and offer suggestions for improvements.

> **Systems must be fully understood before they can be improved.** Processes often involve many people and departments and no one person understands the entire process. Attempts at improvement are often just tampering with a small part of a larger system. Such tampering can have unforeseen and perhaps undetectable negative effects.

> **It's better to understand and improve an entire process than to try to optimize parts of it.** For example, changing delivery routes may save fuel, but it may also be false economy if customers become unhappy with delivery times.

> Structured problem-solving approaches that use teamwork and data analysis work better than "on-the-fly" improvements.

> Graphs aid in the presentation and analysis of data.

> **When things go wrong, look for flaws in the system—not for someone to blame.** Chances are, the system is at fault or at least contributed to the problem. **(Look for the why, not the who.)**

If you want to do a thing badly, you have to work as hard at it as though you wanted to do it well.
—PETER USTINOV

PERSONAL DEVELOPMENT

< *Career Goals* >

I am where I am because I believe in all possibilities.
—WHOOPI GOLDBERG

It's easy to land a job and wish for the best, allowing circumstances or luck to take over until retirement. But a passive, unsystematic approach to advancement and satisfaction at work often leads to countless, unfulfilling days on the job. You can make work both emotionally and financially more rewarding by transforming dreams into goals. Here are some tips:

> **Study your daydreams about work.** They tip you off to your deepest, most genuine desires. Do you daydream about working outdoors? Running a large company? Making things? Owning your own company? Working with numbers? Helping people? Teaching? Traveling? Don't assume that daydreams are automatically unrealistic or unachievable. **If we're serious about a dream, it's attainable.**

> Make the dream a goal. Our hopes and dreams fade because we treat them as dreams instead of reachable goals. **Turn a dream into a goal by spelling out just what it is you want, why you want it, when you want it, and what must be done to achieve it.** Define it in

such vivid terms and in such detail that the first few steps become obvious. Do so in writing because, just as we can't hit an invisible target, we can't reach a vague goal.

> **Identify and anticipate obstacles.** If you dream of practicing law, you must go to law school. Requirements like training, education, credentials, and experience are common. Talk to experts and read to find out exactly what stands between you and your goal.

> Picture success. **Believe and act as if success is inevitable.** Your subconscious will pick up on this positive assertion. It will generate the confidence, talents, and attitudes needed to assist you. A positive subconscious attitude helps notice things that may be useful in reaching your goal. That's why the falling apple meant so much to Newton.

> **Focus.** Set one major goal at a time. Sometimes we want so many things that we prevent ourselves from obtaining the important ones. Working people who want to spend time with their family, write a book, and obtain an advanced degree are probably spreading themselves too thin.

> **Set interim goals and timetables.** We can't reach a goal in one giant leap. Instead of saying "I'm going to write a book," say "I'll write a chapter a month." Instead of saying "I want to be president of a hospital," say "I'll be a vice president in seven years." Your schedule will motivate and help you measure your progress.

> **Anticipate doubts.** You and others may regularly express doubts about your chances of success. Deal with negative comments and

thinking by replacing them with positive affirmations. Instead of thinking "It's unrealistic to believe I can manage an accounting department," think "I have the brains, determination, and plans to manage this department."

> **Be prepared for setbacks.** Plans rarely proceed without difficulties. Assume you'll have occasional disappointments. Expect discouragement and even despair. When those feelings hit, take the long view. Think about your goal and all the reasons it's worth pursuing. Rejuvenate yourself by reading inspirational articles about the difficulties successful people overcame. Remind yourself that you're just paying dues. Press on.

> **Enjoy the process.** Success is a journey, not a destination. Look for satisfaction while you work toward your goals. That way, if circumstances turn against you or you're forced to settle for less than you'd hoped, you can look back on the fun you had along the way.

We grow great by dreams.
—Woodrow Wilson

< *Workplace Blues* >

If all the year were playing holidays,
to sport would be as tedious as to work.
—SHAKESPEARE

No one is immune to bouts of the workplace blues. This malady often strikes without warning, and the symptoms and duration vary. You may suddenly feel trapped in a dead-end job that's boring and burdensome. You may long for a job that more fully utilizes your talents. You may daydream about contributing more to society. Try these remedies for temporary spells of job dissatisfaction:

> **Expect ups and downs.** They're a natural part of everyone's work life. Enjoy the good days, and work through the bad ones.

> **Be realistic.** While you're in the depths of an unpleasant mood, it's easy to think you'll always feel that way. Recognizing such faulty logic can help nudge you out of it.

> Balance the scales. You're probably focusing on the parts of your job you dislike. **Step back and remind yourself of the parts you enjoy.**

> **Look forward to something.** Help weather the storm by thinking about weekend or vacation plans.

> **Tell someone.** Simply telling a good listener you're having a bad day or horrible week can release pent-up feelings.

> Think of your customers. You may not be curing cancer, but you are doing something for someone. **Think of your contribution from your customer's point of view.**

> Do something. **Refresh your outlook.** Take a friend to lunch, read an inspirational article or book, watch an upbeat movie, or do athletics. Resist the urge to sit around and brood.

> **Recount successes.** If things haven't been going your way lately, your self-esteem may be low. Lift it by reminding yourself of your personal strengths and past successes.

> **Consider the long haul.** If the workplace blues keep coming back and you genuinely believe you're in the wrong job, chart a new course. Explore your likes, dislikes, strengths, and weaknesses. Learn about the big world out there, and find a more appealing and rewarding niche.

I've developed a new philosophy. I only dread one day at a time.
—CHARLIE BROWN (CHARLES SCHULZ)

< *Performance Reviews* >

Win without boasting. Lose without excuse.
—YOGI BERRA

Students know how well they are doing in school. Grades on home-work, tests, and report cards keep them informed. Such frequent on-the-job feedback is rare. It may even be limited to formal annual reviews in which your boss discusses your performance with you.

The performance review is the equivalent of a report card. It's usually a written record of how well your bosses think you're doing, and is important because it is often used in determining raises, promotions, and layoffs. With the right strategy, you can use the performance-review process to your advantage. Here's how:

> **Get a copy of the form your boss will use in the meeting with you.** Study the categories you'll be graded on. They'll probably include knowledge of job, attitude toward work, quality of work, creativity, initiative, interpersonal skills, and communication skills.

> **Find out when you'll be reviewed.** Don't assume it will be at the same time as other employees. New employees may initially be reviewed more frequently.

> **You may want to talk to your boss about the form.** Find out which categories are most important to her.

> **Concentrate your efforts on the categories that are most important to your boss for the position you hold.** In a bank, accuracy is important. In an advertising department, creativity may be stressed.

> **Keep a summary of your projects, activities, and accomplishments.** Add to it routinely or you'll forget what you've done by the time of your performance appraisal. Concentrate on things that may have increased sales or decreased expenses. Companies like bottom-line results.

> Save complimentary letters and memos.

> **Rate your own performance, using the performance-review form.** Do it months before the real thing, and try to see yourself as your boss does. If you're not particularly impressed with your score, start an improvement plan.

> Your boss may be reluctant to offer ongoing constructive criticism. If so, seek informal feedback from him. Ask questions like "How could I have done this better?" or "Is this the way you would have done it?" or "Would it have been better if I did it this way?"

> Your boss may be required to review many people. If there's a chance that your accomplishments will be forgotten or minimized, remind her. A brief memo a few weeks before the review will help refresh memories.

> **Be confident, not defensive or emotional, during the review meeting.** It is not designed to find fault. Don't leave the meeting until you understand what your boss thinks of your performance, what is expected of you in the future, and how to improve it.

> **Develop a plan to exceed the duties of your job and your boss' expectations.** It's the first step to a promotion.

A bad review is like baking a cake with all the best ingredients and having someone sit on it.
—DANIELLE STEEL

< *Presentations* >

It's natural to have butterflies.
The secret is to get them to fly in formation.
—WALTER CRONKITE

Making a presentation to management, customers, employees, or the public offers the opportunity to shine and improve your reputation. Some tips:

> **Know your subject.** There is no substitute for a thorough understanding of the topic. Do your homework until you feel ready to do a professional job.

> **Know your audience.** Tailor your talk to them. If they know little about the topic, don't use jargon. If they are knowledgeable, don't talk down to them.

> **Know your purpose.** Is it to inspire, persuade, entertain, or instruct? Design your approach to fit that purpose.

> Organize your material into an introduction, main body, and summation.

> **Rehearse.** Being knowledgeable is not enough to impress your audience. Make sure you can communicate in an understandable, cogent, confident manner. Rehearse with particular attention to the beginning and end of your presentation because those sections

are likely to make the biggest impression. Also rehearse answers to the questions most likely to be asked.

> Be friendly, not pompous. **Aim for an easy, natural manner that makes your audience feel as if you're talking to them as friends.**

> **Use stories.** Everyone enjoys listening to a story and wondering how it will end. Stories that entertain and help make your point are sure to help keep the audience interested.

> **Be sure of pronunciations.** If in doubt about a word's meaning or pronunciation, look it up. Make sure you also know how to pronounce the names of those who are introducing you or speaking with you.

> **Arrive early.** Make sure things such as lights, chairs, visual aids, and room temperature meet your needs.

> Mingle. **Greet your audience as members arrive.** This helps put you at ease and gives you familiar, friendly faces to look at as you speak.

> Keep visual aids covered. Uncover them at the appropriate time, otherwise your audience may be distracted. Cover them again after they've served their purpose.

> **Open your presentation with confidence.** Avoid uncomplimentary remarks such as "I'm not very good at this" or "I put the last audience to sleep." Your first few sentences are likely to set the mood for the entire presentation. Choose them carefully. Aim for

an opening that grabs the audience's attention and makes them want to listen.

> Mention the basics. **Mention logistics, such as how long you plan to speak and whether you plan to take a break.** Give directions to rest rooms, phones, and restaurants if appropriate.

> Be sincere, enthusiastic, and humorous if applicable. **Make eye contact with your audience.**

> **Repeat questions from the audience to ensure everyone heard them.** If you don't know the answer, don't fake it. Say you're not sure, but you'll find out.

> **End decisively.** Signal the end of the presentation with a phrase such as "in closing" or "to sum up." End on a high note, and thank your audience for their attention.

I've never thought my speeches were too long: I've enjoyed them.
—HUBERT HUMPHREY

< Asking for a Pay Raise >

Who timidly requests invites refusal.
—SENECA

Many factors influence how much employees are paid. These include the general economic climate, size of the company, union rules, and longevity. In addition, employees with good negotiating strategies and skills earn more than those without them. Here are some tips on negotiating pay raises:

> **Don't get personal.** Don't try to use your personal financial situation to justify an increase. **Business is business.** It's immaterial that your car needs major repairs or your spouse was laid off.

> **Don't give an ultimatum.** Saying "If you want me to stay here, you'll have to pay me more" may work under unusual circumstances, but it identifies you as a disloyal mercenary, and it may backfire in the long run.

> **Pick the right time.** Don't ask for more money in the wake of mistakes you've recently made. Synchronize your request with a string of good results or favorable remarks from customers. It also helps if the company itself is doing well.

> **Understand the marketplace.** Most employers pride themselves on treating employees fairly. Find out how your pay compares with similar positions in your organization, industry, and geographical area. Use this knowledge to avoid forming unrealistic expectations

or making unreasonable requests. If you're at the low end of the scale, be sure it isn't due to your performance.

> **Have concrete justification.** Bring examples of how you've decreased expenses, increased sales, maintained customer loyalty, and gone beyond the call of duty. You may want to bring written notes you can share with your boss. It helps to write down your achievements as they occur so you always have a ready list.

> Describe your plans. **Present your boss with your written plans, goals, and objectives for the next six to twelve months.** Explain how the company will benefit from your efforts. Make the boss eager to keep you and reward you for your initiative and continued high performance.

> **Suggest options.** Compensation can be increased in ways other than pay. If appropriate, suggest a company car, bonus, computer for doing work at home, better health-care benefits, and similar forms of remuneration.

> **Be prepared for rejection.** Have responses ready in case your request is denied. Even if you plan to look for another job, don't reveal your plan. Ask what you can do to earn a pay raise. More education? Additional responsibilities? Better performance? Promotion? If you make no headway, ask to discuss the issue again after an appropriate time.

> **Be patient.** You may not get the raise you want, but you may have succeeded in getting the boss to think about you and your value to the company. This may result in a larger pay increase next time.

> **Consider moving on.** This should not be a rash or last-resort move. It should be part of your overall career strategy. If better long-term opportunities exist elsewhere, take a hard look at them. Keep in mind that people who move a few times in their career usually earn more than those who stay with one employer.

I'm living so far beyond my income
that we may almost be said to be living apart.
—E. E. CUMMINGS

< *Readable Writing* >

*This report, by its very length, defends itself
against the risk of being read.*
—WINSTON CHURCHILL

A surefire method to impress your boss is to write direct, straightforward, easy-to-read, easy-to-understand letters, memos, and reports. How an idea is presented is often as important as the idea itself. Weak, disorganized writing can make a great idea seem confusing. **Clear, strong writing helps sell good ideas.**

First, a word of caution. The written word tends to have greater significance than the spoken word. Criticism, sarcasm, and even jokes can easily come across too strong. Face-to-face conversation benefits from voice inflection, body language, facial expressions, eye movements, and the general mood of the situation. So don't put everything in writing. If it could be easily misinterpreted or held against you, think twice before putting it on paper or in someone's electronic mailbox. **The written word can be damning evidence.**

Some writing tips:

> Get organized. Before putting pen to paper (or fingers to keyboard), plan. **Make sure you know who your audience is, what you want to tell them, and the order in which you want to say it.** Some writers swear by written outlines. Others won't touch them. But everyone agrees that planning is a valuable investment. If ideas occur to you before you start, jot them down.

> **Use the correct format.** Your company probably has formats for letters, memos, and reports. Find out what these are, and use them.

> **Get to the point.** Long introductions and lengthy explanations are hard on readers. So plunge right in. State your point early to let the reader know what this will be about. Make them want to read on.

> "Talk," don't write. It's not true that long, flowery writing and big words impress readers. Busy people don't want words to get in the way of ideas. **Shoot for simple, clear language.** Avoid an artificial style. Instead, try for a friendly talk with your reader. Oh yes, it's OK to use contractions and personal pronouns. (We can't do without them.)

> **Gain momentum by pouring it out.** Once you've written the first word, keep going. Write every idea, phrase, and sentence that comes to you. Just keep writing and don't go back to edit or criticize yourself. Ideas often generate more ideas. Surprisingly often, we come up with ideas we didn't know we had in us. And don't stop the flow to find that special word or phrase. Leave a blank space and fill it in later.

> **Don't exaggerate.** It makes readers question the validity of everything you tell them.

> **Make a report visually appealing.** Use wide margins, brief paragraphs, and bullet points (the way this book is written). Consider emphasizing important words by underlining or using a boldface font: <u>like</u> **this**. But don't overdo it because it can distract readers.

> **Vary sentence length.** Readers tend to get lost in sentences more than twenty words long. An average of fifteen or so is good. But include an occasional short, snappy one. Get it?

> **Revise.** Drafts are usually just a group of ideas strung together. Use two steps to improve them. First, make sure the ideas are organized in some way. It could be order of importance. It might be chronological. Second, take a good look at paragraphs, sentences, and words. Here are some things to look for:

> **Use the active voice:**

- *Betsy led the meeting.*   NOT   *The meeting was led by Betsy.*

> **Avoid "fancy" words:**

- *given*   NOT   *disseminated;*
- *explained*   NOT   *delineated;*
- *pay*   NOT   *remuneration.*

> **Use specific, concrete words that picture details:**

- *rain*   NOT   *unfavorable weather;*
- *broke his leg* NOT   *was injured;*
- *he cried*   NOT   *showed unhappiness;*
- *station wagon* NOT   *car;*
- *book*   NOT   *publication.*

> **Use short, snappy sentences:**

- *That's life.*   NOT   *Things in people's lives go wrong.*

> **Remove extra words:**

- *if*   NOT   *in the event that;*
- *after*   NOT   *subsequent to.*

> **Avoid noncommittal language:**

- *I think*   NOT   *it is the opinion of the author;*
- *he distrusted*   NOT   *he did not have confidence in.*

> **Use a friendly tone:**

- *sure I'll go*   NOT   *it will be a pleasure to attend.*

> **Remove hackneyed phrases like:**

- *on account of;*
- *in the event that;*
- *each and every;*
- *in order to;*
- *at this point in time.*

> **Read it aloud.** Make sure it "sounds" good.

> **Revise again.** If you have time, put your writing aside. Weaknesses surface after simmering overnight.

> **Proofread.** But not right after you've finished because you're likely to see what you expect to see. If time permits, wait a few hours before proofing. It's also a good idea to have someone else check what you've written. Be especially careful that personal names are spelled correctly. (The best way to find typos is to read a report after you've distributed it.)

> Do not send out paper that is wrinkled, has coffee stains, or otherwise presents a poor image.

> **Learn by reading good writing.** Study the style and structure of writers you admire, and mimic them.

> *Be obscure clearly.*
> —E.B. WHITE

< *Losing Your Job* >

A lot of fellows nowadays have a B.A., M.D., or Ph.D.
Unfortunately, they don't have a J.O.B.
—FATS DOMINO

In today's economy, everyone is susceptible to layoffs. Losing a job is one of life's most stressful events. **An action plan can reduce the stress and help you obtain a better severance package.** Here's one such plan.

Before the bad news:

> **Be realistic.** Despite excellent performance reviews, steady pay raises, and a great relationship with your boss, you could lose your job. Thousands of talented, hardworking employees fall victim to mergers, acquisitions, new competition, and industry downturns every year.

> **Be watchful.** Keep an eye on the financial health of your industry, the competition, your employer, division, and department. Also evaluate the status of your boss within the organization. If his position is under siege, you could become a casualty as well. If the future looks uncertain or bleak, decide whether it is best to weather the storm, change jobs within the company, or look elsewhere. In any case, always have a contingency plan.

> **Be prepared.** Visualize how you'll react when you're told your services are no longer needed. Develop a plan to take the offense and negotiate a good severance package. A strong, confident reaction

and a detailed plan of attack will probably catch your employer off guard and strengthen your negotiating posture.

When you're told the bad news:

> **Stay calm.** An emotional outburst will only work against you.

> **Accept the bad news.** Layoffs are serious matters, and your employer no doubt gave this decision much thought. Pleading to be spared is counterproductive.

> Ask for a minute to gather your thoughts. You're likely to be shocked by the news and hear only bits and pieces of what is said. **Ask for time to compose yourself and get a pencil and paper for notes.** Leave the room if necessary, and return once you have composed yourself.

> **Negotiate.** You may have a stronger hand than you believe. For instance, your employer probably feels awkward and guilty about the situation. Also, how you're treated will affect the morale of other employees. In addition, it may be helpful to have you as a friend in your new job. So, don't be shy about asking for a better severance package than is offered.

> **Understand the details.** Discuss lump-sum or installment severance pay, health insurance, dental insurance, life insurance, disability insurance, vacation pay, pension, professional membership dues, magazine subscriptions, company car, unemployment benefits, retraining, and other facets of your relationship with your employer.

> **Ask for help.** Some companies hire firms to help their laid-off employees find new jobs. Try to make such outplacement and counseling services part of your severance package. If that fails, ask to use the company's secretarial services and photocopier to type and copy résumés.

> **Get it in writing.** Although your employer is probably not obligated to provide a separation package, it is a common practice. Push for a written summary of your severance package, and sign only those documents you fully understand. Seek legal help if necessary.

> **Agree on an announcement.** Suggest who—you or your employer—should tell your coworkers you've lost your job. Agree on what will be said.

> **Know your rights.** Seek legal advice if you believe you are the victim of age or sex discrimination. Contact an Equal Employment Opportunity Office for guidance.

After it sinks in:

> **Be professional.** You may or may not get a chance to return to your office or workstation. In either case, do not bad-mouth your employer to other employees. **Do not burn bridges.**

> **Apply for unemployment insurance.** The stigma, long lines, and atmosphere of the unemployment office will probably make you uncomfortable. Swallow your pride, and confidently obtain the financial help owed you.

> **Expect emotions.** Unemployment causes strong emotional reactions. Your will likely feel angry, frustrated, victimized, and even depressed. **Accept your reactions as normal, and work through them.** Commiserate with others who have lost their jobs. Seek professional help if the struggle is too difficult.

> **Be honest with yourself.** Reflect on your work life. **Did you cause your job loss?** Did you fail to do things you should have done? Did you do or say things you shouldn't have? Can you learn from this experience and use it to your long-term advantage?

> **Be optimistic.** Granted, losing your job is a terrible experience, but it happens every day to thousands of people. Like them, you'll pick up the pieces, move on, and find a new job. Who knows what the future holds? Perhaps you will look back on this event as one of the best things that ever happened to you. We hope so.

When prosperity comes, do not use all of it.
—CONFUCIUS

MOVING UP

< *Networking* >

The dog that trots about finds a bone.
—Spanish Gypsy Proverb

When many people know you are looking for a job, you stand a good chance of getting "lucky" and landing the position you want. **Networking means systematically contacting everyone you know to ask for help, advice, and support in your job search.** Surveys indicate that many, many jobs are filled through such informal, personal contacts. Here's how to use this powerful job-seeking strategy:

> **Get serious.** Looking for a job and networking require determination, initiative, and persistence. **Finding work is your full-time job.** Stick to a regular work schedule or you'll fritter away your time and miss opportunities. Don't tell yourself you'll look for a job after you wash the car, watch a movie, or exercise. Do those things after "work" hours.

> Get organized. **Have an "office" and be in it on time every morning.** Use a spare bedroom or a corner in the basement. Have a phone and office supplies.

> Understand networking. It isn't asking for a job. It's done to get job-hunting tips, leads on job openings, and names of other people

to contact. **Most importantly, be sure that many, many people are aware of you and your search.** You want them to think of you when they hear that the job of your dreams just became available.

> Be prepared. Others must know about you and the kind of job you seek before they can help. Offer a concise, informative description of your education, interests, technical skills, talents, abilities, experience, accomplishments, and career hopes and plans. Prepare answers to questions that are likely to be asked.

> **List contacts.** That means everyone you know, including friends, relatives, members of your place of worship or other organizations, schoolmates, neighbors, and local businesspeople. The larger the list, the greater your chances of success.

> **Organize your list.** Since you may talk to many people during your search, it will be easy to forget conversations and details. Put names and phone numbers on paper large enough to contain lots of neat, easy-to-read notes.

> **Don't be bashful.** It's easy to think no one will be interested in helping you find a job. People who have looked for a job (and who hasn't) know what you're going through. Many will help for that reason alone. Many will be flattered that you asked for their help. Others will be glad to talk about their industry and share their expertise. Some will talk to you as a favor to a mutual friend or business acquaintance. Many will do you a favor in the hopes that you may be able to return it someday. Remember, most people are friendly and helpful.

> Rehearse your initial conversation. Keep your tone light, friendly, and confident. **Ask for a face-to-face meeting because it's difficult to make a powerful impression over the telephone.**

> **Rehearse your meeting.** Since you asked for the meeting, it's up to you to lead it and make sure you accomplish your objectives. Be confident, clear, concise, and make a good impression. Be ready with opening lines and questions that will keep the conversation going. Ask for the names of other people to call. Take notes. Ask permission to use your current contact's name when you call. Make sure everyone knows how to contact you in case they hear or think of something promising. **Hand out printed business cards with your name, address, and phone number.**

> **Send a thank-you note.** Convey your appreciation and mention how you'll use what you learned in the meeting.

> **Stay in touch.** Let your contacts know you're still in the job market, as well as how your search is going. Notify them when you find a position, and thank them again.

> **Continue to network.** Contacts and good relationships are important in the working world. Cultivate the relationships you developed during your job search, and continue to expand your circle of acquaintances.

Character and personal force are the only investments
that are worth anything.
—WALT WHITMAN

< *Moving On* >

We must change to master change.
—LYNDON B. JOHNSON

Everyone occasionally thinks about changing jobs. Most of us will do it voluntarily several times. Reasons may include increased pay, better benefits, new geographical location, better chances for advancement, or difficulties in the current job. No matter the reason, it's a major decision. Some tips:

> Cool down. **Don't quit in a huff.** You may be tempted to tell off the boss or walk off the job. No good can come from it. Never willingly make an enemy of employers. Someday you may need them as a reference, contact, or even as a customer.

> **Don't slack off.** Maintain the quality and quantity of your work. Your reference will be based largely on your most recent performance. In addition, you may change your mind and decide to stay. A slump in your performance could cost you a pay raise or even your job.

> **Be discreet.** Announcing your plan to look for another job diminishes your stature in the organization. Employers are unlikely to promote or invest training in employees who may not be around much longer. Such an announcement makes you expendable.

> **Discreetly learn about your fringe benefits.** It could be to your advantage to use some of your vacation time. You may have four

weeks in your vacation bank, but your employer may pay you for only two weeks when you leave. Understand your other benefits, especially health insurance. Make sure you understand your coverage as you change from one job to another. Check on the vesting date of your pension plan. If you are close to becoming vested, understand the financial implications of leaving before you are.

> **Be selective.** Don't accept a job offer simply because you are desperate to leave your current position. Concentrate on finding something better.

> **Don't feel guilty.** Leaving an employer usually means ending several good relationships with co-workers and even bosses. Don't let that stand in the way of finding better opportunities. You have no reason to feel guilty if you've given your best to your employer.

> **Be professional. After you have accepted a new position, write a letter of resignation.** Say nothing negative in it. State that your decision is based on personal career goals. **Give appropriate notice.** A rule of thumb is one week's notice for each week of vacation you're entitled to. Give longer notice if your vacation payout or other benefits depend on it. Mention that you'll complete as much work as possible in your remaining time.

> **Don't burn your bridges.** (Armies burn bridges behind them so the enemy can't follow. However, this strategy has a major disadvantage: the army itself can't turn around and go back, because the bridges are gone!) Leave on good terms with your boss, and resist the temptation to be "honest" with her during an exit interview or during your last few days on the job.

> **Remain on good terms.** Consider calling your former boss after a few weeks to see if there are loose ends you can help with via the phone. It's a thoughtful way to keep in touch and demonstrate your professionalism.

Never continue in a job you don't enjoy. If you're happy in what you're doing, you'll like yourself, you'll have inner peace. And if you have that, along with physical health, you will have had more success than you could possibly have imagined.
—JOHNNY CARSON

< *Index* >